Praise for *Elephants Befo*

More money goes into bureaucratizing the workforce than inspiring the millions of people who turn up to work hoping to be able to do a good job each day. If more organizations paid attention to the lessons of this book, they would find both their work and their lives transformed.

—MARGARET HEFFERNAN, CEO AND AUTHOR OF *WILLFUL BLINDNESS*

In *Elephants Before Unicorns*, Caroline Stokes does an enlightening job of bringing emotional intelligence to the hiring, onboarding, engaging, developing, and leading aspects of people in organizations. Starting from her own frustration in big brand organizations, she followed her heart to discover the magic of what makes great organizations so special. There's a lot you can use here to help transform your organization for the better. And it might save you some of the frustrations Caroline went through to get there.

—STEVEN J. STEIN, FOUNDER AND EXECUTIVE CHAIRMAN OF MULTI-HEALTH SYSTEMS, CO-AUTHOR OF *THE EQ EDGE: EMOTIONAL INTELLIGENCE AND YOUR SUCCESS* AND *THE EQ LEADER*

In the advent of AI and robotics, fears abound about the future of work. Drawing on her vast experience as a business coach, Caroline cuts through the doom and gloom and offers an uplifting view of the next industrial revolution. In this informed, practical guide she demonstrates how tackling "elephants" or oft-invisible obstacles, while developing emotional intelligence is critical to success in an AI future. I recommend her book to people leaders who want to lean into their power and shape a future-forward workforce.

—CHRISTOPHER YOUNG, VP OF ENTERTAINMENT CREATION PRODUCTS AUTODESK

Want to get ahead in the talent wars? In *Elephants Before Unicorns*, Caroline Stokes has created a wise, practical success manual for modern leaders. If you seek to build talented teams—and ensure your organization thrives in the age of AI—pick up this book now.

—Dorie Clark, author of *Entrepreneurial You and Stand Out*, and adjunct professor Duke University Fuqua School of Business

Caroline Stokes' *Elephants Before Unicorns* is a must-read for business leaders. What worked for companies in the past will not work for forward-thinking organizations hoping to attract and retain the superstars of tomorrow. With humor and heart, Caroline brings her experience to bear in sharing how companies can win the war for talent and thrive in the AI age.

—Marshall Goldsmith, *New York Times* bestselling author of *Triggers*, *Mojo*, and *What Got You Here Won't Get You There*

With *Elephants Before Unicorns*, Caroline Stokes brings her years of experience, emotional intelligence and must-learn lessons for business giants. In a time where hiring the right players for your team has never been more important, this book has the winning formula for any and every hiring decision. I recommend you ride this wave with Caroline and watch the magic happen.

—Ian Curran, president and COO of Sega of America

Elephants Before Unicorns is a must-read for organizational leaders, from CEOs to stressed-out recruiters. When it comes to transforming the *how* and *why* your organization finds talent, every organization has problem areas holding us back from potential greatness. Caroline does a wonderful job of helping us discover and address these elephants in our own organizations so we can all thrive!

—TIM SACKETT, PRESIDENT OF HRU TECHNICAL RESOURCES
AUTHOR OF *THE TALENT FIX*

A mindful organization starts with mindful leaders. *Elephants Before Unicorns* is an invaluable resource for leaders who want to evolve their companies' emotional intelligence and create a happier workplace for their teams.

—JACQUELINE CARTER, PARTNER AT POTENTIAL PROJECT INTERNATIONAL
AND AUTHOR OF *THE MIND OF THE LEADER: HOW TO LEAD
YOURSELF, YOUR PEOPLE AND YOUR ORGANIZATION FOR
EXTRAORDINARY RESULTS*

Stokes, Caroline,
Elephants before
unicorns : emotionally i
[2019]
33305246910693
mi   12/27/19

elephants
before
unicorns

Emotionally Intelligent
HR Strategies To
Save Your Company

caroline stokes

Entrepreneur Press®

Entrepreneur Press, Publisher
Cover Design: Andrew Welyczko
Production and Composition: Eliot House Productions

© 2019 by Entrepreneur Media, Inc.
All rights reserved.
Reproduction or translation of any part of this work beyond that permitted by
Section 107 or 108 of the 1976 United States Copyright Act without permission of the
copyright owner is unlawful. Requests for permission or further information should
be addressed Entrepreneur Media Inc. Attn: Legal Department, 18061 Fitch, Irvine,
CA 92614.

This publication is designed to provide accurate and authoritative information
in regard to the subject matter covered. It is sold with the understanding that the
publisher is not engaged in rendering legal, accounting, or other professional services.
If legal advice or other expert assistance is required, the services of a competent
professional person should be sought.

Entrepreneur Press® is a registered trademark of Entrepreneur Media, Inc.

Library of Congress Cataloging-in-Publication Data
 Names: Stokes, Caroline, author. | Entrepreneur Media, Inc., publisher.
 Title: Elephants before unicorns : emotionally intelligent HR strategies to save
  your company / by Caroline Stokes.
 Description: Irvine, California : Entrepreneur Media, Inc., [2019] | Summary:
  "Elephants Before Unicorns is for overcoming "elephant" obstacles and building your perfect "unicorn" company culture. Bringing her expertise from HR
  to EQ, Caroline Stokes offers business owners the actionable strategies they
  need to gain and retain a quality workforce"-- Provided by publisher.
 Identifiers: LCCN 2019019961 | ISBN 978-1-59918-658-0 | ISBN 1-59918-646-2
 Subjects: LCSH: Employee retention. | Personnel management.
 Classification: LCC HF5549.5.R58 S86 2019 | DDC 658.3/01--dc23
 LC record available at https://lccn.loc.gov/2019019961

Printed in the United States of America

23 22 21 20 19   10 9 8 7 6 5 4 3 2 1

To my husband, David Harries, for frequently telling me I could write a book, even before I knew that I wanted to write a book. His vision of my capabilities, encouragement, patience, and support are more than I could have wished for from my life partner and the father of my children. And many thanks to my rapidly growing young adults, Jasper and Felix, for continually understanding my love for the work I choose to do and making way for me to do it. Thanks, home team!

Contents

Foreword
by Darrell M. West
Author of *The Future of Work:*
Robots, AI, and Automation

This is a time of tremendous change worldwide. New digital technologies such as artificial intelligence and robots are transforming major business sectors, from health care and transportation to education and retail. With the aid of emerging technologies, businesses are less likely to rely on traditional employees working in isolation in an office cubicle. Instead, they are automating routine tasks, offering flexible work arrangements, and encouraging teamwork and collaboration.

Yet many workplaces still recruit the old-fashioned way, make decisions in a hierarchical manner, don't understand the kind of talent they need, and are confused about their overall mission. As a result, they make mistakes that drive away key talent and prevent their organization from achieving its full potential. Too often, firms look more to the past than the future for answers.

In this book, Caroline Stokes tackles the crucial topics of how to lead during transformative times and the importance of emotional intelligence in handling current challenges. A noted thinker with a background in corporate communications, strategic management, and executive recruitment, she offers keen insights into today's vexing questions:

▶ How do you build effective teams?
▶ How do you break down organizational silos?
▶ How do you deal with a rapidly changing world when conventional answers are no longer compelling?

She proposes an innovative approach based on finding "unicorns." These are people with the ability to manage organizations through challenging transitions. Drawing on a wealth of knowledge from her personal experiences as well as the experiences of those she has coached, Caroline paints a compelling portrait of the types of individuals businesses need today, as well as how organizations should handle a wide range of internal and external obstacles.

The major task facing organizations today, according to Caroline, is overcoming the organizational "elephants" that impede change. Those include people who are ill-prepared to deal with change, company cultures that preclude innovation and risk-taking, organizational routines and structures that slow decision making, and leaders who view feedback as a threat rather than an opportunity. Companies must think carefully about how to deal effectively with these challenges.

This book particularly resonates with me because I have lived through many of the shifts she describes. For example, I wrote my dissertation in the 1970s on a typewriter. I have witnessed the subsequent shift from desktops and laptops to tablets and smartphones. I now lead the Center for Technology Innovation at the Brookings Institution where I analyze technology trends and study how they affect organizations, leadership, and management.

With each advance in technology, I have had to think about how digital tools influence the way people get information, make decisions, and receive feedback from inside and outside an organization. Technology can flatten organizations and improve information flows. Automated procedures and digitized processes can raise productivity, free workers from mundane tasks, and improve the prospects for collaboration. Implemented effectively, AI, robots, machine learning, and data analytics can increase organizational performance and create new opportunities for workers.

However, emerging technologies and the new business processes that come with them also generate a number of risks. They can threaten people, disrupt existing routines, and create employee paranoia about their jobs. Some employees may worry about their place in a changing work force and whether they are still valued by company executives.

It takes time to introduce change wisely and help people see the value of new processes. Managers have to listen carefully to feedback and make adjustments as they go along. Mandating change from on high is rarely effective at transforming organizations. Company success requires managers to demonstrate emotional intelligence—and considerable skill at navigating major obstacles.

This book is filled with compelling examples of what does and doesn't work for leaders dealing with change. Taking advantage of her experiences with major firms and a wide range of leaders, Caroline shows how emotional intelligence shapes how leaders perceive situations, express themselves, relate to others, make decisions, and handle stress. As the global business environment increasingly relies on emergent technologies, having leaders who understand both reason and intuition is vital. Mastering one without the other can undermine effective leadership and management and derail an organization.

Caroline talks in an engaging style about the major elephants organizations must avoid. For example, companies often hire too quickly and without checking on the intangible qualities that are important for leadership and management. Rather than getting sufficient feedback on possible recruits, they let their need for a new hire outweigh their assessment of whether they are getting the right person for the job. That approach often ends with both employer and employee dissatisfied.

foreword by darrell m. west

Some companies devote too little attention to their interview process, sending poor messages in the way they identify talent and structure recruitment. Inadvertently, their processes may signal that not everyone's opinions are fully valued or that their company is not a welcoming place. Devoting some time upfront to thinking about their hiring procedures and expectations and what they want to convey about their organization will yield dividends down the road.

A similar problem arises during the onboarding process. Companies spend a lot of time trying to find the right person for a job, but then often neglect the first 100 days after hiring a new manager. They assume the new hire can figure out their culture and mission by osmosis and learn as they go along. Caroline recommends coaching for new top hires so the onboarding process goes smoothly.

Structuring feedback is also vital in effective organizations. To improve performance and keep workers on track, leaders must provide feedback and open themselves to receiving feedback about their own performance. One of the hardest things for many managers to accept is being open to the views of other people and recognizing that the people they supervise have a lot of wisdom. Having effective procedures for listening and seeing how other people react is crucial for long-term organizational success.

Building an inclusive workplace is indispensable in today's world. The work force is changing quickly and is now made up of a wide variety of people. You will meet older workers, those in mid-career, Millennials, and Gen Y; there are employees of various races, religions, cultural backgrounds, sexual orientations, etc. It can be challenging—but rewarding—to bring people of differing backgrounds together and help them gain the benefits of their diverse experiences.

In addition, re-skilling the team is crucial as new technologies transform the workplace, creating jobs that don't even exist today. And many workers will need new skills to take on additional responsibilities. The old model of investing in education only through about age 25 will give way to lifetime learning, whereby people continue to develop new skills throughout their 30s, 40s, and 50s.

Preparing for an AI future does not have to mean doom and gloom. Incorporating new processes within the organization can create excitement, improve work flows, and make it possible for people to work more effectively with one another. AI and data analytics can improve decision making and position the firm for greater heights. One of the virtues of the digital era is the broad range of information at leaders' fingertips. There must be a way to harvest and analyze that material in any organization. In these pages, Caroline serves as a cheerful guide, inviting us to embrace the possibilities of AI and mold the new technology to our own greatest good.

During a time of extensive change, no company or leadership team can be content that its future is assured. Many prominent organizations have fallen on hard times by failing to anticipate the future and adjust to changing circumstances. Recruiting leaders and managers with the emotional skills to adapt to a rapidly changing environment is one of the most important tasks companies face today.

Contemporary leaders confront many challenges in terms of technology, organizational routines, and geopolitical alignments. Old formulas no longer guarantee success. Hiring leaders with the dexterity to understand shifting circumstances and the empathy to bring people together in a common mission is crucial. Companies that do this effectively will be well-positioned for the future. This is a valuable book for those seeking to comprehend the current environment.

Introduction

"There has to be a better way."

It was my first "big girl" job at Virgin Interactive Entertainment on Ladbroke Grove in London. I was so excited to dive into the working world.

I'd been impatient to get to work all my life. The grownups with business degrees who went to work, solved problems, and made the world a better place—they looked like they knew what they were doing. From the outside looking in, the men and women of the corporate world seemed to have all the answers.

But I soon learned how rose-tinted my adolescent glasses had been. As a young PR executive at Virgin, I realized that the idealized working world of my dreams was nothing like reality. It's not that my colleagues were bad people or that I felt intimidated by the pressures of the job. In fact, I couldn't quite put my finger on the disconnect. I spent a great deal of time searching for the source of my unease, wondering why things didn't seem to fit together as perfectly as I thought they would.

Here we were, members of a giant corporation, given the job of working together to steer our boat over stormy seas. Yet that's not what was happening. I came to see that there were different factions of the organization vying for power. The sales and marketing people acted as if they were superior to the engineers, while the engineers endured the extroverts who surrounded them and then acted out their frustration through passive-aggressive behavior. And I was stuck in the middle—an empath totally distressed by the discord around me. I felt like grabbing my colleagues by the collar and screaming, "Stop! We're all in this together! Why can't we just get along?"

It wasn't just that I was young and naive. I found this dynamic in every organization I worked with throughout the 1990s and 2000s. These workplaces had significant interpersonal issues—yet everyone accepted them. This dysfunction was seen as "just the way it is." And even if people wanted something better, leadership often lacked the basic tools to create cultures of collaboration rather than competition.

Emotional Intelligence: The Better Way

I knew there had to be a better way—a path by which we could put aside our differences, find common ground, and work for the greater good. This was the early 1990s, before Daniel Goleman published his game-changing 1995 book *Emotional Intelligence: Why It Can Matter More Than IQ*. Emotional intelligence (EQ) is something *no one* was talking about back then; the concept was absolutely groundbreaking. When I read Goleman's book, it was like a bomb hitting me. This was it! This was the tool I'd been looking for! How much more successful would companies be with emotionally intelligent leaders at the helm? What if, instead of people feeling compelled to constantly brandish their egos, they were aware of how their emotions affected them? What if people took time for self-examination and could identify where their emotions were helping them and where they were harming them? What if an entire organization took this approach?

It was an idea ahead of its time. Still, the seed was planted, and it was watered and nurtured as I evolved through the 1990s.

We've come a long way. Not just technologically (remember a time before email?), but ideologically as well. Twenty-five years ago, few people were talking about leadership skills or a greater mission. Leadership development was considered a *punishment*. I vividly remember conversations from that era in which colleagues talked about how "everything you needed to know you could get from experience." Studying management techniques, receiving coaching—this was what you did if you were *failing* in your role!

What mattered back then was the bottom line. In some ways, it was an "anything goes" era. We may look back from 2019 in bewilderment that we behaved that way. We've since witnessed such revolutions as the democratization of the internet and the #MeToo era. The game has changed many times since my career began. And now we are on the verge of another great upheaval: the fourth industrial revolution.

This revolution is characterized by the widespread adoption of new technologies such as robotics and artificial intelligence. The three previous industrial revolutions also centered on advances in technology. The first industrial revolution saw societies move from farms to cities as the iron and textile industries expanded. The second encompassed the era of the steel and oil barons, as electric power was harnessed for mass production. The third, also known as the digital revolution, brought humanity the internet and the PC.

And now we stand on the brink of the fourth. Yet the shift we are experiencing runs deeper than the changes society experienced in the previous three revolutions. Those technological upheavals primarily affected how people worked; the end result of each was that labor became more streamlined and efficient. Yet the fourth industrial revolution—a term coined by Klaus Schwab, founder of the World Economic Forum—is larger in scope. It is about more than labor. Technology is a means to an end, and that end is a deeper connection with one another, the internet, and the earth.

Artificial intelligence (AI) will figure prominently in the new work landscape. Machines will become smarter, and humans will interact with them more frequently. The way we think is likely to change, too, as our intelligence merges with the technology we're creating. AI is already changing the way we live and work. We experience it when we click on a website, interact with chatbots, or use it to help doctors diagnose a disease. Within the next few years, it will transform the world. AI has been called the "new electricity." Its impact will be felt by every person, across every industry, in every corner of the world.

What this may mean for your workplace is that employees who perform routine functions will be replaced by automation, while jobs requiring soft skills like empathy and leadership will become more prominent. Technological systems that haven't yet been invented could totally disrupt your processes within two or three years. Though you can educate yourself on which new technologies are coming down the pipeline, there's no way to accurately predict how they will affect you and your organization.

Top Talent Will Make Your Company Resilient

That said, there's no need to cower in fear. But to thrive in the fourth industrial revolution, organizations need to be prepared. Organizations that hope to survive need to attract top talent. The best defense against an unpredictable future is a strong, agile team that can respond to the ever-evolving technological scene. According to a May 2018 discussion paper by management consulting firm McKinsey & Company entitled, "Skill Shift: Automation and the Future of the Workforce," these teams will consist of people with advanced EQ and communication skills.

I call these elusive individuals "unicorns."

Ahh, the unicorn. The mythical creature that symbolizes the connection between physical and spiritual reality. In mythology, the horn of a unicorn has healing powers. Unicorns inspire hope and feelings of unlimited possibility.

When organizations seek out "unicorns" today, they're looking for the same things: magical individuals who will turn a company around, lead an organization as it develops new products or projects, or drive a company through a challenging transition. The chase for unicorns is often frustrating and often thrilling. It's what gets me up in the morning. My professional title may be "executive headhunter," but I'm really a "unicorn hunter." I want to create the perfect match between organization and individual and watch as magic is made.

Yet between company and unicorn, there are large, lumbering obstacles that need to be removed before we get to that match made in heaven. These are the "elephants." At Virgin, the culture of its time was an invisible elephant, standing in the way of the teamwork, collaboration, and innovation I craved. And on a personal level, it stressed me out! When an opportunity to join Sony arose, I chased after it with the naive hope that grass would be greener, like most people who move to a new role and organization.

If organizations understand and demonstrate control of their elephants, talent will want to stay. A company with too many elephants in its path can't see where it is going, and the unicorns it wants to attract can't see the company with great possibility, either. A company dominated by its elephants can't compete effectively—and will likely fail.

But by identifying the problem, we can work toward the solution. Since my first experience in the corporate world, I've made it my mission to help companies become healthier by naming their elephants and finding a way around them. That is the purpose of this book. Chapter by chapter, we'll look at the most common elephants organizations face—the obstacles that are standing in the way of true progress. We'll cover everything from your recruiting team's attitude to employer brand and feedback avoidance, employee disengagement, lack of strategy, and even re-skilling your team. By looking these elephants in the eye (or the trunk, so to speak), you'll be able to see which practices are holding your organization back from true greatness. More important, you can take action to remove them. I'll show you how to engage your emotional intelligence and meet obstacles head-on—until they are no longer obstacles. On the other side of these elephants, your unicorns are waiting.

There's nothing I find more gratifying than helping individuals and organizations evolve. I'm an idealist. I want to make the world better, and I love an interesting challenge. How humanity will adapt to the AI age is the single biggest challenge of our time. As an optimist, I'm not interested in the warnings of a coming dystopia as humans are replaced by robots. There is tremendous potential in this moment, as the very structure of society is rapidly changing. An alternate vision to doomsday—one in which emotionally intelligent humans and artificially intelligent machines work alongside each other for the good of all—is possible.

Tesla founder Elon Musk gives away his patents so that everyone may benefit. As part of his Buddhist practice, world-renowned leadership coach Marshall Goldsmith gives away his knowledge for free. In this book, it is my intention to offer you what I've learned over the years working in the corporate sector and as an executive headhunter and coach—to share my stories, best practices, and useful techniques for evolving yourself and your organization ahead of the fourth industrial revolution. Because what we do *now* determines the future. It's up to us to create the tomorrow we deserve. It's my belief that emotionally intelligent individuals and companies have a key role to play in establishing a flourishing society.

Who This Book Is For

There are leaders, and then there are *people leaders*, and every people leader needs to understand their organization's elephants. Who are the people leaders in an organization? Most obviously, there's the CEO. I believe an emotionally intelligent, conscious CEO is the most significant factor in whether an organization succeeds.

But I take a broader view and define people leaders as anyone who manages people in any capacity. If you have even one direct report—guess what? You're a people leader! And this book is for you. You may not think of yourself as a people leader, but instead as a team leader or project leader. But I want you to embrace the fact that you are, in fact, a leader of *people.* Whether or not you realize it, you have a tremendous impact on the direction and success of your organization. That's good news. I commend you for recognizing your power, accepting the responsibility, and learning what it will take to move your company forward.

No matter where you stand in your organization's hierarchy, I challenge you to embrace the mantle of "leader." Own your influence. Find where you can do the most good, and then do it with all your might. Seek innovative solutions and experiences that will help you grow as a person and as a member of your organization. Your individual commitment to excellence will have ripple effects throughout your company. Excellence is contagious. Lean into and evolve your power.

This book is for you.

How to Use This Book

Now that we've identified your role as a people leader, let's talk about how to use this book. Chapters 1 through 5 deal with the hiring process, from facing the pressure to fill a role to attracting the right person to your team to the onboarding process. Chapters 6 through 14 focus on leading and managing your teams. We'll look at how to spur your teams on to do their best work once your unicorn has signed on with you, how to keep your employees engaged in their work, how to give and accept useful feedback, and how to hire diverse teams. We'll also examine what you need to do as a leader to avoid burnout, make space for creative and strategic thinking, respond to changing work trends in a way that is authentic and beneficial to your organization, and re-skill teams to prepare them for technological advances.

Each chapter will examine which component of emotional intelligence is engaged when dealing with the topic at hand. You may reflect on areas in which your EQ is strong and areas in which you've yet to grow. As a leader of people, you recognize that strengthening your emotional intelligence will benefit yourself and everyone around you. There are practical, actionable tips in each chapter on how you can grow as a leader and learn to work with EQ. We start by recognizing that we are all driven by emotion and feeling, whether or not we realize it. We seek to harness our EQ so that the emotions that do not serve us well don't run roughshod over our lives and work.

You may read each chapter in this book individually as it applies to your situation, or you may read it straight through and let it inform how you think about and prepare for winning the talent wars and attracting the unicorns you need. My hope is that you will be able to refer back to specific chapters as you have need—for instance, you might reread Chapter 10, "Your Workplace Isn't Safe for All Employees," before launching a diversity initiative.

Before we dive into the particulars, however, we need an EQ 101 introduction to the five components of emotional intelligence. Let's dig in!

Chapter 1

Defining Emotional Intelligence

A s important as emotional intelligence is for functioning in a healthy way, people are often fuzzy on what it *is*. They conflate it with emotional awareness: "I feel happy, I feel sad, I feel frustrated," etc. Awareness is a part of the larger whole, but it's far from everything you need to know about emotional intelligence.

The term *emotional intelligence* was coined by social psychology researchers Peter Salovey and John Mayer in their landmark article of the same name, published in the journal *Imagination, Cognition and Personality* in 1990. The term became a part of the cultural vernacular in 1995, when *New York Times* science writer Daniel Goleman published his book *Emotional Intelligence: Why It Can Matter More Than IQ.* Salovey and Mayer defined it as the ability to process one's own emotions and the emotions of others and to use this information to guide decision making and behavior.

When I became an executive coach, I was searching for a tool to help me learn what makes my clients tick: what motivates them and what holds them back. The first time I incorporated emotional intelligence into my coaching using the EQ-i 2.0 assessment (which you'll read about more in the next section), things just clicked. In one session, I got to a deeper level with the candidate as if we'd already been meeting for weeks. *Aha!* I thought. I became an instant fan.

I now incorporate EQ into all my coaching sessions and believe enhancing your emotional intelligence is one of the most important things you can do to be more successful. Even the most self-aware individuals benefit from EQ coaching. None of us can know ourselves with perfect accuracy. We may have particular areas that continually trip us up and cause frustration, yet not understand *why* these pain points keep arising.

As an EQ coach, I can help candidates see ways to improve their EQ. For example, I may ask, "Hmm, your stress management score is low. Do you have strategies to help you deal with anxiety? No? Well, what are some things you enjoy doing? How could you schedule those into your week?" After strategizing together, the candidate incorporates this new plan into their work week. As a result, her stress management capabilities increase, she becomes more productive at work, and she is better able to work with others and accomplish key goals. Consider this book my coaching session with you.

In this chapter, you will learn about the five categories of emotional intelligence. As we examine different elephants in the workplace later in the book, you'll see which EQ categories become stressed in different scenarios—and you'll learn how to bring awareness to each situation so you can navigate the best path forward.

The Five Components of Emotional Intelligence

Emotional intelligence, as measured in the Emotional Quotient Inventory (EQ-i 2.0) is composed of five categories, each with three subcategories as shown in the following sidebar.

MHS EMOTIONAL QUOTIENT INVENTORY (EQ-I 2.0)

1. *Self-Perception*
   - ▶ Self-Regard: Respecting oneself; having confidence
   - ▶ Self-Actualization: The pursuit of meaning, self-improvement
   - ▶ Emotional Self-Awareness: Understanding one's own emotions

2. *Self-Expression*
   - ▶ Emotional Expression: Being able to constructively express emotions
   - ▶ Assertiveness: Communicating feelings and beliefs in a nonoffensive manner
   - ▶ Independence: Being self-directed, free from emotional dependency

3. *Interpersonal*
   - ▶ Interpersonal Relationships: Able to maintain mutually satisfying relationships
   - ▶ Empathy: Quality of being understanding, appreciative of how others feel
   - ▶ Social Responsibility: Developing a social conscience, helping the larger community

4. *Decision Making*
   - ▶ Problem Solving: Ability to find solutions when emotions are involved
   - ▶ Reality Testing: Ability to be objective; see things as they really are
   - ▶ Impulse Control: Ability to resist or delay the impulse to act

5. *Stress Management*
   - ▶ Flexibility: Adapting emotions, thoughts, and behaviors
   - ▶ Stress Tolerance: Coping with stressful situations
   - ▶ Optimism: Maintaining a positive attitude and outlook on life

Copyright ©2011, Multi-Health Systems Inc. All Rights Reserved. Reproduced with permission from MHS.

Let's break down each of these elements so you can begin to apply them to your own company.

Self-Perception

How you perceive yourself colors your interactions with the rest of the world. Thus, *self-perception* is the first category identified in the EQ-i 2.0 assessment. *Self-regard* makes up the first subcategory. The confidence and respect you have for yourself impacts your decisions and communications with others. *Self-actualization*, the second subcategory, concerns your pursuit of meaning and self-improvement. If you are fully self-actualized, you have become the "largest" version of yourself—someone who is fully living out what you view to be your life's purpose. The third subcategory is emotional self-awareness. Being aware of your emotions is not self-indulgent. Rather, it's necessary for healthy and happy living. Repressed emotions manifest as sickness, disagreements with others, constant anxiety, and a host of other unpleasant symptoms that hamper your ability to live and work at the level you seek.

Self-Expression

Your perception of yourself influences how you express yourself. *Self-expression*, the second component of EQ-i 2.0, comprises three parts. The first is emotional expression. Once you are aware of your emotions (as noted in the *self-perception* category), you must be able to express them. Healthy individuals can express their emotions and take responsibility for them without blaming others. Assertiveness makes up the second part of *self-expression*: Can you communicate your feelings and beliefs in a way that causes no harm to others, yet honors your desires and needs? And the third and final component is independence. If you are independent, you are self-directed and free from emotional dependency on other people. You maintain steadiness regardless of the moods or opinions that are prevailing around you, and you do not require validation from others.

Interpersonal

The first two categories of EQ-i 2.0 are concerned with the self. The third deals with how the self interacts with others. *Interpersonal relationships*, the first subcategory, addresses how you can adapt your ability to evolve and adapt all relationships from the meaningful people in your life to how you impact others. The second subcategory is *empathy*, meaning how well you can be understanding and appreciative of how others feel. Without empathy, a satisfying *interpersonal relationship* cannot form. The third subcategory is *social responsibility*. This builds on the previous two concepts: If you have positive, empathetic relationships with other individuals, you can then expand your consciousness and strive to help the larger community, both locally and globally.

Decision Making

Pop science claims the average human makes about 35,000 decisions each day. An emotionally intelligent person can make decisions with less inner turmoil. The first subcategory of *decision making* is problem solving: Every time we make a decision, we have to tackle a myriad of emotions to reach a solution. When we understand our own emotional cycle, we can hijack the approach and improve our decision-making skills. The second is reality testing. If you have strong reality-testing skills, you can be objective and see situations for what they really are without getting caught up in made-up stories, magical thinking, or worst-case scenarios. The third subcategory is impulse control. In a people leader, a lack of impulse control can do serious harm to organizational morale. Say a CEO is a sucker for new technologies, so he invests in the newest and best tools—every six months. Employees must continually learn and adapt. As soon as they master one system, here comes another. They're victims of the boss's "shiny object syndrome." By contrast, a CEO with strong impulse control carefully considers the technologies available, chooses the best option for his company, and sticks with it.

Stress Management

We all have stressors in our lives, but we can choose how much they affect us. Have you ever known someone who flies off the handle at the smallest provocation—say, if the coffee pot is empty? Then there's the person who lives like he's in the eye of the hurricane: The whole world could be falling to pieces around him, yet he retains an almost unnatural calm.

Flexibility, the first subcategory of *stress management*, refers to your ability to adapt your thoughts and behaviors to a given situation. It's how you respond and react in the moment. It's about the hundreds of course corrections you make throughout the day to maintain emotional steadiness. Stress tolerance, the second subcategory, encompasses how well you cope with stressful situations. Reflect honestly on yourself: Are you closer to an "eye of the hurricane" person, or a "coffee pot freakout" person? The answer will give you insight into your level of stress tolerance.

The third subcategory is optimism, or how well you maintain a positive outlook on life. Optimism breeds resilience. If you have a healthy baseline level of optimism and you encounter setbacks, you have confidence that things will right themselves in time. All is not lost.

View Your Company Through the EQ Lens

These five categories of emotional intelligence serve as a useful barometer for people leaders in the workplace by helping them identify the source of tension or stress. Where discomfort and tension exist, you can peel them apart and see which component of EQ is under stress. No one acts with perfect emotional intelligence all the time. You are a human being subject to stressors both in and out of the workplace that can inhibit how you communicate with others. Perhaps you get a lousy night's sleep. Maybe an invaluable team member quits out of the blue, or you blow out a tire on the way to work. These pressure points can throw you off your game, taxing your reserves of patience disproportionately.

Yet you can gain clarity when you look at your life through the lens of these five categories of emotional intelligence. Ask yourself: What exactly is causing my discomfort? You may find that the situation in question has dealt a blow to your *interpersonal relationships,* making you feel disconnected from the larger mass of humanity (both in and out of the workplace). Or perhaps you feel that you can't be who you really are or say what you need to say—your *self-expression* component is out of alignment. Rather than judging yourself for these lapses in emotional intelligence, you can get curious about the cause.

You can see that these five components of emotional intelligence are not silos. Rather, they're linked. A gap in one area will likely affect the functioning of the other four, thereby inhibiting your effectiveness as a leader. You needn't fear. You need only to be aware of where the problem lies.

Throughout the rest of the book, as you read about each elephant through an EQ lens, I'll be referencing these categories and subcategories. My goal is for you to consider how the elephant is affecting you and your team so that you can enhance your awareness and be alerted to any blind spots you may have. After reading this book, you will have a fuller understanding of two things: how your emotions are helping and harming you, and how they may be influencing your direct reports and affecting your employer brand.

You're reading this book because you recognize the importance of enhancing your emotional intelligence to grow your business. There's a lot at stake here! We know that companies that don't adapt will not survive. I want you to not just survive, but thrive. So begin by bringing awareness to the problem (the elephant), and then consider how you can best adapt yourself and your organization to solve it.

You don't need a Ph.D. to increase your emotional intelligence. You can start right where you are (with this book in hand) to become a more effective leader and create a healthier work environment.

The following chapters examine 14 elephants commonly found in organizations. These elephants are present at every stage in the company: from pursuing potential unicorns to the interview process, onboarding new hires, and giving and receiving feedback to teammates—and then all the way up to the C-suite, where we examine how company leaders can most effectively guide their teams through periods of transition. Elephants are experienced differently by individuals within the organization, depending on their roles. An elephant in one area may be a reflection of a larger elephant somewhere higher up the company chain.

For example, say you have an underperforming team. You begin to peel back the layers of the onion and get to the heart of the problem. A closer examination reveals that the manager is uncomfortable giving and receiving difficult feedback. Star team members become frustrated, but they don't know how to address the gap between the manager's tepid feedback and the team's clear problems. The superstars take on more than their due, and before long, they burn out and leave. A feedback elephant has thus morphed into a disengaged-employee elephant. When employees leave, a heavier burden is placed on recruiters, and if you've got elephants in your recruiting, you have a problem on three fronts now. Everything is interconnected and impacts everything else.

This is why it's so important for company leadership to regularly take the pulse of the organization and see where elephants exist. Quite simply, becoming an emotionally intelligent organization is great for business. Talent is your number-one resource, so when you make your organization irresistible to employees, everything else is enhanced. Your products are stronger. Emotionally intelligent organizations consistently perform better on their key performance indicators (KPIs) and objectives and key results (OKRs). But to achieve that goal, you must first take stock and see where you stand now. In the next chapter, you will learn how to best diagnose how you can impact your company EQ so you can address the elephants lurking in your business.

This diagnostic has three sections. Part one will help you recognize your weak spots in talent marketing, or "unicorn attraction." For example: Do your unconscious biases (the unexamined, under-the-surface attitudes you have toward certain groups of people) inhibit the hiring process? If they do, your organization could be missing out on some megawatt talent. Part two focuses on the employee experience. How engaged are your employees? How do you *know* they're engaged? Finally, in part three, you'll examine how effectively your leadership team is working together as you face the future and adjust for a changing marketplace.

No company is perfect. Growth is the goal. As you begin this journey, remember that progress, not perfection, is what counts. Each day—each moment—brings with it a chance for incremental improvement.

Let's begin.

Chapter 2

Discover Your Elephants: Workplace Diagnostic

Before you start identifying the elephants that are dragging your company down, you need to understand your EQ. The process of increasing emotional intelligence starts with you and the other people leaders in your company and then filters down to teams and individuals. By diagnosing your leadership's EQ, you can:

▸ See which areas of EQ you need to improve to lead most effectively.

▸ Gain insight into team dynamics.

▶ Provide other leaders with accountability as you all seek to grow your EQ, and receive accountability for your own growth.

▶ Clarify how leadership dynamics affect workplace function.

Let's say, for example, that the CEO and CFO of your company are constantly at odds. On the surface, the cause of the conflict appears simple. The CEO has grand ideas; the CFO claims they're not in the budget. After conversations with the CEO, the CFO comes away frustrated. He does not feel that he can express himself or that the CEO understands where he is coming from. The CEO, by contrast, is constantly annoyed by what she perceives as the CFO's "small-minded thinking."

Both take the EQ assessment. The CEO scores very low on impulse control, while the CFO scores low on assertiveness. The assessment does not say that either the CEO or the CFO is a "good" or "bad" person. It merely provides information to help both gauge their current EQ.

With this information in hand, the CEO and CFO are able to have an honest conversation. The CEO acknowledges her impulsiveness and recognizes how it must frustrate the CFO, who has the budget to worry about. The CFO talks about the difficulty he feels being assertive and commits to speaking up more. He asks the CEO for support in this so he can feel heard in their conversations. The CEO agrees. Going forward, the two can relate to each other from a heightened place of understanding.

A healthy leadership team with highly developed EQ lifts the entire organization. It's like the old adage: On an airplane, put on your oxygen mask before helping your seatmate. People leaders must first tend to their own EQ development if they're going to help their organizations become healthy. Once they have a healthy baseline level of EQ, only then can they tackle their company's elephants. If your EQ is not where it needs to be, I highly suggest hiring a coach who can help you evolve.

In this chapter, I will walk you through some simple diagnostics you can use to get a feel for where your company stands in terms of challenges. The following diagnostic, shown in Figure 2.1 starting on page 11, is designed to help you and your fellow people leaders identify your company's elephants. Once you do that, you'll be able to attract the type of unicorns your company has always dreamed of.

Workplace Elephants: A Diagnostic

Take a few moments to answer the following questions. Each question may be answered with either a "yes" (Y) or "no" (N). Give yourself 1 point for every "Y" and 0 points for every "N."

Part 1: Unicorn Attraction

Question	Yes	No	Total
1. We're aware of the selling points of our employer brand. We know which reasons employees cite most often as their favorite reason for working here.			
2. Our recruitment strategy reflects company ideals.			
3. Recruiters have been trained to evolve their emotional intelligence. We have a system that measures how candidates experience recruiters, either positively or negatively.			
4. Our onboarding process has been evaluated in the past six months with feedback from recent hires.			
5. Recruiters and hiring managers undergo regular professional development from industry experts.			
6. Selling points of the employer experience and brand are marketed across all recruitment platforms.			
7. We use technology to correct for unconscious biases in recruitment and interviewing.			
8. Multiple people are involved in the interview process for thoroughness of background checking and as a check against the hiring manager's unconscious biases.			
9. Our employee retention rate is improving.			
10. We learn and improve from employee exit interviews.			
Total			___ out of 10

FIGURE 2.1—Workplace Diagnostic

Part 2: Employee Experience

Question	Yes	No	Total
1. We've invested time and money in training to make our workplace more inclusive, OR we have definite plans to do this in the future.			
2. Employees are empowered to give feedback, no matter their position.			
3. We have a growth mindset toward employees and enjoy supporting their advancement.			
4. Each member of the organization can state the company's mission.			
5. Beyond once a year, there is a system by which managers regularly give and receive feedback from their direct reports.			
6. Managers own their strengths and weaknesses and communicate these to their direct reports.			
7. It is safe for team members to say, "I made a mistake."			
8. We continually strive to improve the employee experience.			
9. Team members are connected to their "why" for working at the company.			
10. Salary is discussed openly in the interview process and throughout the employee experience.			
Total			__ out of 10

FIGURE 2.1—Workplace Diagnostic, continued

Part 3: Company Leadership

Question	Yes	No	Total
1. All new key hires receive coaching from someone outside the organization.			
2. When leadership has plans to implement new technology, each interested party can say why the technology is valuable and will help us meet our goals.			
3. Leaders are encouraged to regularly engage in activities that help them de-stress.			
4. We're aware of changing market trends that will likely impact our industry.			
5. We're aware of stress points in our work force (emotional, financial, physical, etc.) and are working to address these.			
6. We have a plan to adapt to the changing marketplace and can explain why this plan is the best course.			
7. The C-suite is answerable to the larger organization. We have a culture of openness.			
8. We regularly tell our employer brand story internally.			
9. Everyone in the organization knows the organizational values; these values guide decision making.			
10. Leaders have a clear sense of how their work is contributing to social advancement.			
Total			__ out of 10

FIGURE 2.1—**Workplace Diagnostic,** continued

Total score: _____ out of 30

Unicorn Magnet: A score of 23 or higher shows you're creating a happy, meaningful work experience for your employees and will most likely have strong teams in place as you grow. Congratulations! You just need to leverage some blind spots and define your next steps.

On the Verge: A score of 16–23 indicates that while you have some way to go in clearing the elephants from your path, you're aware of what you need to do.

Gaining Traction: A score lower than 16 means you have some key elements in place to establish your company as an emotionally intelligent organization ready to attract unicorns and grow, but you have a way to go to get there.

FIGURE 2.1—**Workplace Diagnostic,** continued

Now look back at your scores. Which section is strongest? Which is weakest? To attract and retain talent, see which areas are holding you back. If you've got a long way to go toward becoming a unicorn magnet, start small. Focus on one area at a time—whichever is most pressing for your situation. Growth begets growth: When you enhance one area, the rest will follow.

If you're further along, don't just keep playing to your strengths. Instead, target your organization's weaknesses and work as a group to influence experimentation and change. As you go, be ever mindful of these three core areas of company health and seek ways to foster continuous improvement, one small step at a time. The reward is becoming an emotionally intelligent organization able to attract and retain top talent, who will in turn move your company forward.

Finally, if you want to fast-track your own professional and interpersonal development, I highly recommend you take the individual EQ-i 2.0 assessment with an EQ-i 2.0 practitioner. It's the fastest way to get a clearer sense of your own strengths and growth areas. Then, as you read this book, you can loop back and see how you are playing into patterns that make your workplace an emotionally healthy or unhealthy environment. With enough awareness and practice, you can form new, healthier instincts that will benefit yourself and your colleagues. For more resources, visit https://www.theforward.co.

Now that you have some idea of where your elephants may be lurking, let's start unpacking some of the most common corporate elephants. First up: your hiring process. We'll examine how to slow down without grinding to a halt so you can get the right person in the right role. We're aiming for nothing less than a perfect match between unicorn and company—one in which both parties give each other an enthusiastic "Yes!" before signing on the dotted line.

Chapter 3

Elephant: Your Hiring Process Is Too Fast

"We need this position filled sometime, but there's no rush. Take your time and be sure you find someone who's the perfect fit."

Does that sound familiar? Of course not!

When there's a talent gap in your company, you want it filled pronto, especially if you've just lost one of your unicorns. You have objectives to meet, projects to implement, and new products to launch. These require all hands on deck collaborating, innovating, and putting in long hours. When a valuable team member leaves for a new opportunity, it can be devastating for team and company morale, as well as the bottom line.

So what happens when you have a role you need filled yesterday? Traditionally, the process looks like this: The CEO consults with the hiring manager, who contacts recruiters. Everyone is stressed. The CEO and hiring manager want the position filled quickly. The recruiter wants to get paid. Speed is prioritized—how quickly can the recruiter come up with a warm body to fill the chair? That's a little overstated, but let's face it—finding a warm body is often the basic strategy when it comes to attracting talent.

Hiring managers and recruiters will deny this. But with pressure coming from the top (it *always* starts at the top), stress is transferred to the hiring manager and then to the recruiter. And people who are stressed do not make good decisions.

The result is that undesirable characteristics in candidates are overlooked. The hiring chain does not take the time for thoughtful consideration. Instead, they are ruled by their impulses and biases. A candidate is rushed through the process as quickly as possible. In the off chance that it works out—great! No need to read further. You may pat yourself on the back and thank your lucky stars that you happened to chance upon a unicorn.

But that's not real life, is it? Unicorns aren't found by accident. In the real world, rushed hiring decisions have drastic consequences. According to Capital One CEO Richard Fairbank, "Companies that spend 2 percent of their time recruiting and 75 percent of their time managing their recruiting mistakes don't have the right people." Thinking only for the short term creates serious long-term consequences.

When discussing hiring tips, Richard Branson coined the phrase, "It's better to have a hole in your team than an asshole in your team." "Hire slow, fire fast." These phrases have been trotted out so much that they're almost clichés. But in the face of looming deadlines and mounting pressures, it's hard to know what to do.

In this chapter, we'll examine resources you can use to ensure you are doing your due diligence when it comes to hiring. You'll learn how to make fewer recruiting mistakes so you can focus on attracting the best people and nurturing them so they can do their best work. First things first: Start by managing your stress so it doesn't affect your team.

Manage Stress and Enlist Help

If you want to avoid a costly hiring mistake, you first need to be aware of your own stress level. *Stress leaks.* I say that a lot because it's so important. People leaders need to be aware of how their own stress is affecting their decision-making abilities and in turn affecting those around them. A conscious people leader with strong *stress management* skills (the fifth component of emotional intelligence) can identify when and how stress is impacting his ability to see things clearly. When he has practices in place that allow him to step away from his daily tasks and clear his mind, he can come back to work with renewed energy and fresh insights (more on that in Chapter 13).

Second, don't try to handle the hiring process alone. No matter how much you trust your gut and believe yourself to be a good judge of character, you need many people to weigh in on important hiring decisions. Other people can see where you have blind spots and act as a check on any biases you may have. Ask for the input of hiring managers and the candidate's future team whenever possible. When that input differs from your own opinion, resist the temptation to push the candidate through anyway. Sincerely thank your team members and take their concerns seriously. Many a hiring mistake has been avoided thanks to a brave employee who dared to challenge the higher-ups on a toxic but convincing candidate who interviewed like a superstar.

Use a Pre-Interview Checklist

To alleviate some of the stress of the hiring process and make sure your team is well-supported, take stock of the people and process involved in the decision. Before interviewing for a key hire, all invested parties need to be 100-percent onboard. Forging ahead without the full participation of stakeholders will tank morale and hurt your bottom line. Following is a checklist for you to consider before you begin the hiring process. Don't move forward until you can answer each question.

1. Who can be in your board of interviewers to help make the right hiring decision?
2. What's the process?
3. Is everyone on board?
4. Is everyone aware of the hiring and onboarding timeline?
5. What happens if you don't meet the hiring deadline?
6. Have you discussed your Plan B with the board of interviewers and stakeholders?

Remember: the more communication, the better. If a stakeholder is fuzzy on one or more of the checklist questions, go slower. Losing time in the hiring process will be worth it if you can find a unicorn. You may hear team members say, "We need to move fast to get this person." That may or may not be true. If the prospective employee has a number of offers on the table, then you really do need to move fast. But if she's currently employed, she will leave her job with the same diligence as you are performing in hiring her.

Just remember that the match made in heaven works both ways. If the person you want to hire feels as passionately as you do about your organization, she'll express it. You'll know you're her priority because she believes in the team and the organization. And that means you've got the right person for the role.

Why "Go with Your Gut" Isn't Good Enough

"Go with your gut" has serious limitations. We know how our intuitions and first impressions can be informed by our biases. However, you can't ignore your gut completely—it's your early warning system. Pay attention if your gut is telling you that something is "off" about a candidate. For instance, does he sustain eye contact for longer than is normal or appropriate, making you uncomfortable in what you suspect is an attempt to be domineering? That's a red flag. In the reception area, does the candidate seem so absorbed with herself—looking at her phone, checking her appearance, etc.—that she has little awareness for others sharing the space, or does she speak rudely to employees? That's a red flag. Does the candidate put down or subtly undermine former team members or bosses during the interview? Major red flag.

No matter how stellar a candidate's resume or track record, you must listen to your early warning system. Any interviewer worth his salt will tell you that. First impressions are crucially important. If your gut is sending "danger" signals about a candidate, there's likely no need to pursue her further.

But what about the people you're unsure about? Here's where the sales saying, "The fortune's in the follow-up," applies. Don't simply rely on your own impressions; follow up with as many people as possible. Have the candidate's potential team members spend some time with him—they can go out to lunch, for instance, and see how he behaves away from the boss. Follow up with past supervisors. (Incidentally, did the candidate only give the names of friends or peer colleagues as references and no higher-ups? That's another red flag.) If you have people in your network who know the candidate, however informally, ask for their opinions, too. Someone with the greatest distance from the hiring situation may have the sharpest insights to offer on your potential superstar's character.

Use an Interview Toolkit: Questions and Processing

While you should trust your gut instinct, you need more data to help guide the hiring process. The following questions in Figure 3.1 on page 22 are a resource for you to use both in the interview and afterward. The first set are for the interviewee. They're designed to offer insight into how the candidate prefers to work, what kind of company culture he hopes to find, and what team health looks like to him.

The second set of questions in Figure 3.2 on page 22 are for you to consider, along with your key stakeholders, after the interview. They are a safeguard against simply going with your gut. The person leading the hiring process may create a document in which the board of interviewers all have input. For each question, have the interviewers list positives and negatives.

Aim for honest, collaborative discussion and consensus. All parties should feel comfortable moving forward with the candidate before the hiring manager calls with the offer.

1. What's your ideal product to work on? How would you lead it?

2. What's your ideal team to work with? How do you know when things are going well?

3. What culture do you thrive in? What culture do you yearn for?

4. How do you interpret the role? What do you see as the opportunities and the challenges?

5. Your project has received a green light. How do you proceed?

6. What do you need from me to be successful for this role?

7. What would your colleagues tell me you need to be successful for this role?

8. What does a healthy team look like to you?

FIGURE 3.1—**Interview Questions for Candidate**

1. How would this candidate fit within the culture?

2. How do you see this candidate reaching the goals of this role?

3. How will this candidate deliver the vision?

4. How will the candidate enhance the team?

5. What do you expect the candidate to achieve in 90 days and in one year?

6. What stood out in your interview that others should know?

7. How did the candidate identify *their* vision for the role?

FIGURE 3.2—**Post-Interview Questions with Stakeholders**

Ask References the Hard Questions, Then Listen (*Really* Listen)

Let's say the candidate, "Jim," aces the interview. When you call his references, you want to ask questions that will give you a sense of Jim's character. That means you can't rush the phone call: You must give the person on the other end time to carefully consider his response and express himself fully.

Be alert to any long pauses. Most people are polite and don't want to bad-mouth even the worst former employees. Also be wary if you ask about Jim's ability to work well with others and get an answer like, "It depends on the people." Such a response could be covering a myriad of sins— bullying, sexual harassment, etc. Obviously, if a reference says something that directly contradicts what your candidate said in the interview, that's a serious problem. Below is a reference check toolkit you can use to guide you through even the toughest conversations.

Reference Check Toolkit

Below are the questions I use when calling references. In these conversations, I strive to be exceedingly professional: pleasant, to-the-point, and courteous. I write down exact quotes and do not paraphrase. Then I share what I've written with the reference to give them the chance to correct any misunderstandings. Ask these ten questions:

1. What is your name, title, and current role?
2. What was your relationship with the candidate, e.g., manager, peer, co-worker? When did you last work together? How long did you work together?
3. What are the top three strengths the candidate possesses for this role?
4. Can you describe their leadership and management style?
5. Can you describe their decision-making style?
6. Can you tell me about a time they had to handle extreme pressure?
7. Can you recall the top areas in which the candidate needed to continue developing?
8. If you were in a position to work with this candidate again, would you?
9. What are the most interesting things to know about working with the candidate over time that would not come out during an interview process?
10. Is there anything else you would like to share?

You can learn so much more from a phone conversation than you ever could from a written reference. Listen for pauses, careful word choice, changing the subject, answering a question other than the one that was asked, etc. If a reference is totally glowing, push for more information about areas in which the candidate may continue to grow. If you then decide to hire Jim, you're in an even better position to help accelerate his growth.

The Emotional Intelligence Factor

Let's examine this situation in light of emotional intelligence. The need to hire quickly strains the fourth component of emotional intelligence: *decision making*. If you're stressed, you're less able to *problem solve* (the first subcategory of *decision making*). Your *reality testing* is also compromised—rather than seeing a potentially problematic candidate for what she really is, you look through rose-colored glasses and try to shoehorn her into a role that's not a good fit. *Impulse control* is also weakened; instead of taking the time you need to thoroughly reflect on and vet the candidate, you're ruled by the need to act now. Or, on the other side of the spectrum, you might overcomplicate the problem, which leads to analysis paralysis.

All CEOs and hiring managers could likely point to experiences in which they've made grievous hiring mistakes, either by rushing the choice or by being paralyzed from making a decision. It happens; we're all human. You're likely familiar with the world of problems caused by hiring the wrong candidate. On a bottom-line level, there's the high cost of employee turnover. There are hundreds of studies about the dollars and cents of this. A 2012 study by the Center for American Progress, for example, showed that it cost a business about 20 percent of an employee's salary to replace him.

There's also the stress that a bad hire places on your teams. That new hire you hoped would save your product, department, or company may have just had an inflated ego and ability to talk with confidence—but the real problem is that he is riding on the accomplishments of those underneath him, a surefire recipe for fomenting frustration and resentment. Maybe that candidate you dismissed as "a little brash" when she spoke rudely to your receptionist is simply a jerk. Now the entire team has to endure her rudeness. Perhaps you were dazzled by a candidate's Ivy League education and impressive resume, yet he has little expertise or ability to do the job for which he was hired.

Now you've taken an already stressful situation and created more tension. Your teams, first tasked with meeting KPIs without their departed team member, now have to deliver *in spite of* the new hire. You've placed yourself in the difficult position of having to fire someone because of your own bad judgment, and you've lost credibility along the way. It's a supremely uncomfortable situation for you, distressing for your teams, and unfair to the person you've brought onboard.

Remember, hiring people who can deliver on your company's goals and vision is your most important job. If people are your most valuable asset, it's worth it to put in the time to make sure you've got the right ones on your teams. Failing to do this will sink your ship faster than anything else.

Don't let the elephant of feeling pressured to hire too quickly get in your way. If you keep moving down the path—even if you feel like you're moving too slowly!—you'll get to the true unicorns sooner or later.

▶ QUESTIONS FOR REFLECTION ◀

Hiring the right person (hopefully a unicorn!) takes time. While you may experience great pressure from leadership to fill an empty chair with a new hire, put on the brakes and make sure you and your team are doing your due diligence before making an offer. Ask yourself:

▶ Have I thoroughly vetted the top candidates?

▶ What is my process for connecting with references? Does it work for us?

▶ Do we need to ask more in-depth questions that speak to a candidate's way of working, as opposed to basic level of experience?

▶ How do I use my gut instinct? Have I been burned before? What can we learn from that?

▶ Do we have enough recruitment team members assisting with our hiring process? Does this create a less stressful environment for our team?

Chapter 4

Elephant: No One Likes Your Recruiters

I remember the first time I was contacted by a recruiter. I was at Virgin, putting in long hours every day in an environment that didn't suit my personality. I was a workaholic in what seemed to be a toxic environment, approaching burnout at the beginning of my career. The working world wasn't what I'd thought it would be.

Then a phone call came through to my desk: "Hello, Caroline, I've seen all you're doing at Virgin and would like to tell you about another opportunity . . ."

The recruiter spoke fast. He had to. This was the pre-internet era, and recruiters hustled even more than they do now. To get past reception, the recruiter had to lie—he would never have been put through to me if he had said his goal was to lure me away from Virgin.

"Job XYZ would be a fantastic opportunity for you," he continued. "Are you interested?"

Was I? I scarcely knew how to respond. The entire conversation was a complete surprise. Here I was, plowing away at Virgin, nose to the grindstone. Yet someone had noticed! I felt both shocked and gratified.

"Well . . . no," was all I could muster after several moments. "I'm not interested in another opportunity at the moment."

I wasn't actually sure whether that statement was true, but the open-plan office seemed far too quiet to continue talking. Besides, I had my ever-present to-do list and the uncomfortable sensation that this phone call was making me look conspicuous. I needed to get back to my job.

The recruiter reacted with shock, which threw me into even more of a muddle. *I didn't even know about this opportunity five minutes ago, and now you're stunned I didn't leap at it?*

Little did I know then how frequently that conversation would be repeated over the coming months. The unexpected phone call to my desk, the rushed voice of a recruiter. "Caroline, I see the great things you're doing at Virgin. I have another opportunity that may interest you." It was like being flagged down on the street by random suitors: "Hey there! Want to go on a date with me?" I don't know anyone who's found romance that way, and it didn't work for me when it came to jobs. Even though I was unhappy at Virgin, I found the recruiters who came calling so distasteful that I didn't bite at their offers.

After each "no," the recruiter was as quick to end the conversation as he had been to begin it. "All right, thanks." Click. Rather than feeling gratified, as I had after my first recruiter phone call, subsequent calls left me feeling cold. The hustle became so clear. They were playing a numbers game, not a human game. I felt cheap. The recruiters had zero interest in me personally—they cared only about hitting their quotas for the month.

What a wasted opportunity. Remember, I was unhappy at Virgin! Had a recruiter shown the slightest interest in me as a person and really cared about what *I* wanted, I might have left much sooner.

Times have changed drastically since the early 1990s when I was first being courted. Thanks to the internet, individuals can be contacted upwards of ten times a *day* by recruiters. It's exhausting. Though the methods by which recruiters contact candidates have changed, the end result is often the same: Candidates end up feeling used.

The people you approach to join you deserve better. In this chapter, we'll talk about how your recruiters can keep the delicate recruiter-candidate dance enjoyable—something that ultimately benefits everyone. We'll also talk about how the higher-ups can model emotional intelligence so that their stress doesn't leak to recruiters and then transmit on to candidates.

How the Recruiting Landscape Has Changed—And How It Hasn't

The recruiting landscape has changed very little since my time at Virgin for several reasons. First, recall the harried CEOs and hiring managers in a rush to fill a position. They transmit their stress to the recruiter. The internal recruiter wants to satisfy the hiring manager as quickly as possible, or the external recruiter typically needs to reach their commission goals so they can pay their bills next month—she is not thinking of the well-being of the candidate in this scenario. It's often all about how quickly she can get a body for the open spot and collect her check.

Second, recruiters' attitudes suck. We'll talk more about this in the next chapter. No, not *all* recruiters. And, as mentioned before, they're not solely to blame. Often a stressed-out, short-tempered recruiter is simply reflecting the attitudes of the hiring manager and the CEO. Yet I believe firmly that recruiters must develop their emotional intelligence if they want to have productive relationships with hiring managers that result in placing the right candidates in the right roles—and, in turn, experience more success themselves. I've met very few recruiters who are interested in this type of personal development. I'm convinced this attitude must change, and I'm making it my mission to change minds on this front.

But I'm getting ahead of myself. You need to attract the best talent to your company. A recruiter will provide your would-be unicorn with the first taste of your employer brand. It's a big job, and there's a lot at stake: The recruiter must find the right talent, present the opportunity and answer all her questions, and then help her decide to leave her job and embark on a new path. Emotions are high on both ends. The candidate's career trajectory could completely change as a result of that first contact with a recruiter, while the company may gain a superstar who helps them achieve goals beyond their imagination.

A recruiter holds that power. What an immense opportunity! Amid the demands of the hiring manager and the hustle to fill open spots, it's easy to forget this. Recruiters lose sight of the human being on the other end of the line, and when that happens, everyone is worse off. Candidates feel cheapened, recruiters fail to connect authentically, and the hiring manager loses her unicorn; that special spark just isn't there.

Granted, it's hard to maintain the "spark" when a company suddenly needs to scale up by hundreds of people. One recruiter I spoke to recently had 150 roles to fill. How do you manage a job like that? From advertising a position to onboarding, there are so many tasks that must be done. The recruiter must advertise the role and then somehow manage all the streams of information coming in through social media channels. Then she must narrow the search and actually speak to the candidates. For this task, the recruiter must have an intimate knowledge of the organization. A candidate may have dozens of questions about the ins and outs of the company. The recruiter, like a patient matchmaker, must do her best to answer truthfully while still presenting the organization in the best possible light. There are so many opportunities for the flame of interest within the candidate to be snuffed out. The candidate-recruiter-company dance is delicate, and sometimes it lasts for months. Throughout all this, the recruiter must maintain genuine enthusiasm for and interest in the candidate.

The Recruiting Dance

It's all a dance. Think of dancing with your high school sweetheart or playing "Ring Around the Rosie" as a child. Then, you were carefree and enjoying the moment. But when a recruiter's stress leaks into the process, the dance is no longer a dance. Without the human element, the recruiter's job becomes joyless. Roles must be filled pronto. Hiring managers must be answered to. It becomes all about how quickly the recruiter can finish the job rather than about the people whose lives will potentially be changed forever as a result of the placement.

This is the wrong approach. A recruiter should have enough awareness to realize that, at the end of the day, *it's not about them.* This is not meant to diminish the recruiter. It's actually liberating! It can relieve you of enormous amounts of stress. The recruiter's job is ultimately about persuading someone to leave her job for a new opportunity. Therefore, whenever a recruiter is on a call with a candidate, he presents the opportunity and answers any questions the candidate may have as best as he can. Then he puts the ball back in the *candidate's* court.

I start the recruitment dance with something I call the "coach approach." I developed this technique while undergoing my coaching certification. It's a remarkably simple method that encourages open communication and requires engagement from the candidate (as opposed to the recruiter driving the conversation). I begin each conversation with a question: "How would you like this conversation to start?"

I teach this technique wherever I go, whether at the Society for Human Resource Management (SHRM) or other recruitment events. It's a great joy to watch conference participants role-play with this conversation starter. With this one opener, participants become more open and connected in their conversations. I find that beginning the recruitment dance with this simple question can achieve a collaborative, meaningful conversation that gets to the heart of what the candidate wants.

But here's the key to making it work: The recruiter must be genuinely curious. The recruiter's agenda must not override his desire to help the candidate find the best way forward. For the coach approach to work, the recruiter must be 100-percent committed to the candidate's highest good—whether or not that good lies with the company they're recruiting for or elsewhere. Pressure needs to be taken out of the equation.

*No Pressure—*Really

In my work as an executive headhunter, I've found that taking the coach approach is absolutely essential in matching the right person with the right opportunity. I present the role to the candidate, and then I put my coaching hat on and ask, "How would you like to proceed?"

That's it. Again, I've removed the onus from me by asking a simple question. Ultimately, *it's not about me.* "How would you like to proceed?" places me in a posture of openness and generosity instead of a combative, high-pressure posture. I want to move forward with the candidate, of course. But if I try to ram someone through so I can move on to the next item on my to-do list, I'm setting both him and the company up for failure.

If a recruiter pressures someone into moving further along in the process than he's ready to go, she is taking the candidate's power away. The person the recruiter is meant to serve feels cornered. If the candidate does end up going along without enough time to explore all his options—if he feels disempowered in the process—it will impact his engagement to the point that he'll be looking for the exit sign from day one of his new job (either consciously or subconsciously). "How would you like to proceed?" gives the power to fully engage to the candidate.

How to Not Unconsciously Drive Your Best People Away

A certain retail giant comes to mind when I think about how easy it can be to drive your best people away. When said retail giant (which shall remain nameless) comes courting, it has a horrendous track record of managing candidates. Engineers are contacted multiple times by different recruiters via emails that are one or two lines long. "We'd like to interview you for this position." Repeat, repeat. There's no warmth and no acknowledgment that the same email previously came through. Candidates' first taste of the company's culture is thus a sour one—they're treated as numbers, as pawns to be inserted into vacant positions. As a result, I know many very talented people who declare that they will *never* work for this company.

One example is my Canadian friend Mike. A few years ago, he wrote a screed against this company on his LinkedIn page that went viral. At the time, Mike had a header at the top of his LinkedIn page directed at the company: PLEASE DON'T CONTACT ME. He had publicly boycotted the company based on their treatment of employees and business practices. And yet their recruiters continued to contact him on a weekly basis. Mike shared one of these recruiting emails, which began cheerily: *Hi Future Employee!* The email went on to explain how Mike needed to take a coding test within 48 hours. If he passed, he could travel to one of the engineering hubs at a specified time for the in-person interview. If he passed the interview and was hired on, he would have a choice of working in either Los Angeles or New York.

This email missed the mark on so many levels, it's no wonder Mike grew frustrated. There's the greeting—*Future Employee?* How about using his name? Next, the email gave him "homework": *take this coding test before you've talked to any human within our organization even though your schedule is probably jam-packed.* It might as well have said that, at least. Then, there is the invitation to attend the in-person interviews, in another city, a mere 11-hour car ride away! Finally, there is the line about getting to choose between two American cities. So if he does his "homework," travels 600 miles for the in-person interview, and gets hired—if he does all that, *then* he gets to uproot his entire life and choose between two cities where he most likely knows no one and where the cost of living is outrageous (both cities are in the top ten highest cost of living in the U.S.).

There's an enormous gap here. I asked Mike the other day if he still gets contacted by the company's recruiters. Amazingly, the answer was *yes*.

If the company *really* wanted to hire Mike, they would choose another tactic. Someone senior could reach out and offer to take him out for coffee or lunch. From there, they could have an honest conversation and ask, "What are we doing wrong? What can we do to make it better?" Even if Mike didn't end up signing on the dotted line (which he wouldn't—he's made that clear), such a conversation would be enormously helpful for the organization. There's a reason recruiters keep reaching out to Mike, even if their approach is entirely clueless. He's a phenomenal cryptocurrency leader with experience across all the hot markets over the past 20 years. He could be hired by any top company in the blink of an eye. Any company in this situation would be wise to listen to what Mike has to say and change their approach in recruiting others like Mike.

When an organization has thousands of employees, it can sometimes be hard to teach a giant new tricks. But that doesn't mean *you* and *your* organization can't learn from this example.

A simple human touch goes a long way. There are so many little things recruiters can do to enhance the candidate experience—it's not rocket science. Remember candidates' names and the details of their lives. Be respectful of their time; call when you say you will; don't ask candidates to be available all day for a phone interview (even the refrigerator repairman has more respect for their time than that!). Follow up with candidates, even if the position has already been filled, rather than simply ghosting them. When speaking to a candidate, do your homework. Don't ask questions the candidate has already answered thoroughly.

These are basic reminders of how to treat people with courtesy. Yet they will improve the candidate experience immensely. As a company's first unofficial PR person, recruiters can enhance the employer brand. Kind, courteous recruiters inspire trust and create portable relationships—a connected, engaging conversation during a cold call with a candidate can evolve into a relationship that lasts for years. Even if that candidate doesn't turn out to be the unicorn the company needs right now, she might be the perfect match in a few years' time.

The Emotional Intelligence Factor

From an emotional intelligence perspective, there's so much going on during the hiring process. From the *stress-management* sphere, the recruiter must be aware enough to manage his own emotions and make sure he is not leaking stress that's coming from a hiring manager or CEO. From an *interpersonal* standpoint, *empathy* (there's that word again!) is crucial. The recruiter must employ empathetic listening and be able to truly understand the candidate's feelings. From the *decision-making* component, the recruiter must exert *impulse control* and have patience for the twists and turns of the candidate-recruiter-company dance. The people leader at the company may want everything tied up and ready to go right away. But on the other side, there's a human being weighing his options for the future—considering how a change in jobs would affect his family, retirement, friendships, etc. Even if the recruiter is offering him a seat on the proverbial rocket ship, it's still a *huge* ask. No one can ever afford to lose sight of that.

The recruiter must leave plenty of space for the candidate's emotions as well. It's vital that she allows the candidate to express himself clearly by employing empathetic listening so the candidate can explore his feelings about the opportunity. When this happens—when the candidate speaks openly and is able to make a genuine connection with the recruiter—it's magic. The candidate may say something like, "I shouldn't be telling you this, but . . ." or "I can't believe I'm saying this . . ." These verbal cues are how you know he feels safe sharing with you. They are a signal that the opportunity has registered and the candidate is truly considering the impact it would have on his life and career. The recruiter has managed to connect and enabled the candidate to speak openly about what is most important to him. The candidate has chosen to be vulnerable and is offering that vulnerability to the recruiter. It's a tremendous gift. To quote social scientist and University of Houston professor Brené Brown, "Vulnerability is the birthplace of innovation, creativity, and change." Amazing things can happen when you reach this place of open sharing in a conversation.

Furthermore, the recruiter must give the *candidate* space to exercise the decision-making component of emotional intelligence. The candidate must work through his emotions and be able to objectively look at the situation and determine if the new opportunity is a good fit. Stressed people don't make good decisions. When recruiters take a high-pressure stance and try to shoehorn a candidate into a specific role, they're creating stress around a decision that ought to be made with as clear a head as possible. It's bullying, frankly, and I believe it should be criminal. In this era in which candidates have so many choices so frequently presented, recruiters should *never* adopt the pushy, urgent, and self-serving tone so common in the pre-internet days when they had to con their way through reception to reach a candidate's direct line. Such an attitude is highly inappropriate—yet recruiters too often behave this way all the time.

As a CEO or hiring manager, your recruiters give potential unicorns their first taste of your employer brand. How do you want candidates to feel after coming into contact with a brand ambassador?

▸ QUESTIONS FOR REFLECTION ◂

Not sure how your recruitment practices measure up? Below are some questions for company-wide reflection. Place yourself in your recruit's shoes and imagine that you are coming into contact with your company for the very first time. Engage your curiosity and take an honest look at your recruitment strategy. Where can you make it more human? Remember: The more you infuse your recruitment practices with humanity, the more you will attract quality candidates. Think on these questions:

▸ How do you want candidates to feel after coming into contact with a recruiter from your company?

▸ How personal are your people leaders' outreach methods? Do they have a corporate, cookie-cutter style? Is there a strong human element?

▸ Are you targeting talent with care? (Beware the Mike/large corporation dynamic!)

▸ What do you need to do to create a more human-centered and purpose-oriented candidate journey from first contact?

▸ How are you empowering or disempowering your company evangelists from showing the human side of your company?

No one should feel like a cog in a machine—neither the candidate nor the recruiter. Each party should have the opportunity to appear as their best self. If you infuse your recruitment practices with humanity, you lay the groundwork for an open, trusting relationship between employer and (eventual) new hire.

Chapter 5

Elephant: Your Recruiters Don't Know Their "Why"

A candidate's complex emotions toward recruiters needn't be an elephant standing in the way of your unicorn. As you read in Chapter 4, a recruiter should not transmit stress from the hiring manager and CEO; a conscious recruiter has the emotional intelligence to manage stress and create strong interpersonal relationships with candidates, no matter what pressure is coming from the higher-ups. These recruiters can provide a great experience for the candidate.

But very often, recruiters' attitudes don't match the organization they represent. I've met plenty of recruiters with little to no interest in enhancing their EQ. In short, they don't know why they are doing their jobs. They've lost their way in terms of how their identity relates to the work they do. They have lost their purpose; they have lost their "why."

In this chapter, you'll read about the importance of knowing your own "why" and helping your team rediscover theirs so you can apply it to your search for unicorn candidates. As a jumping-off point, I'd like to share my own "why" story with you.

Finding My Own Why

I came to recruiting "accidentally on purpose." When my second son was born, I gave up my role as a founding partner of a London-based PR agency. I was living in Vancouver, and my newborn had a rare neurological condition. I needed flexibility that my business partner couldn't give me.

Shortly before my second son's birth, a friend had asked me if my husband could refer some racing game talent from Electronic Arts, where he worked as a software engineer. I declined to pass along the request, as there was no way I was going to jeopardize my husband's credibility at his studio. This was before LinkedIn; talent scouting was a lot more painstaking. When my friend asked me to do some headhunting, I shared many ideas on how to find people but ultimately refused. However, I realized that the detective work involved in finding the right person for the role was more interesting than simply giving referrals to someone else and hoping for the best.

I quickly fell in love with headhunting. A new vision started to take hold: I could be a *different* kind of headhunter. I wanted to not just place talent, but to help candidates adapt to their new roles—to provide concierge-level treatment to both the candidate and the organization through a full-service agency. Thus, after much soul-searching—and with a heaping dose of encouragement from my husband—I founded FORWARD in 2013.

From the beginning, FORWARD had three pillars: talent placement and coaching, executive coaching, and recruiter training. That last bit confused a lot of people. Training for recruiters? Was that a wise investment? What was the purpose? What was the "why"?

The business was truly a labor of love. Despite a lot of negative perception, I'd always been intrigued by recruiters (long before I became one myself). A good recruiter must be a scout, a coach, and a confidant. Her job is a service, both to the candidates she is trying to place and to the companies needing talent. Yet it was rare to come across recruiters with a true service mindset. What I saw instead was a lot of chest-thumping bravado, boasting about monthly commissions, and viewing each placement check as another feather in their cap. It was "me, me, me." On the flip side, I saw recruiters who were totally ruled by their stress. When speaking with candidates, these recruiters inclined toward bullying—so desperate were they to relieve their anxiety.

Though the braggart and the neurotic may appear like opposites, these models are two sides of the same coin: at the end of the day, both are ruled by outside forces. Both refuse responsibility for their own emotional intelligence and growth; both have lost sight of the larger picture and the people they're meant to serve. Neither has a sustainable modus operandi. Even the recruiter boasting about his six-figure monthly check is likely to exit the game sooner rather than later. Why? Because human beings are meant to work for more than just a paycheck. We desire work that is meaningful and connected to something bigger than ourselves. If a recruiter sees candidates only as obstacles in the way of a commission check, she'll likely burn out quickly.

At the time, I had a thought I couldn't let go of: "What if people actually *enjoyed* working with recruiters?" I'd encountered such widespread disconnectedness in the recruiters I'd interacted with over the years, but what if things were different? What if candidates could tell the recruiter was actually interested in their well-being rather than merely trying to sell them on switching jobs?

I began to dream up a new goal: I wanted to transform the recruiting industry. I started writing articles on how recruiters could maintain a human-centered approach in their work. I wanted as much content out there as possible so recruiters could truly "get it." Yet I soon saw that I needed to be more explicit about my mission—that it wasn't enough to have an arm of my headhunting agency dedicated to recruiter training. I needed something bigger, but I wasn't sure what.

In 2017, I launched the *Emotionally Intelligent Recruiter* podcast and training platform with the goal of helping recruiters increase their emotional intelligence in the AI age. Finally, people started to get it. With artificial intelligence and deep learning systems taking over large swaths of the recruiter job function—mainly the repetitive bits, such as scanning resumes—it's more important than ever for recruiters to focus on the human-centered part of the job. At the end of the day, humans hire humans. People need someone they trust guiding them through the candidate and onboarding processes.

The Recruiter Satisfaction Gap

At the *EI Recruiter*, my team and I surveyed more than 200 recruiters. Experience levels were pretty evenly split: 50 percent had worked in recruiting for more than 10 years, while 50 percent had been in the game for less than that. Our results were extremely telling (though not entirely surprising). We found that a huge majority—92 percent—dislike aspects of their job. Oft-cited job stressors included communication failures, administrative mishaps, and the repetitive nature of the work. An astonishing 46 percent reported that they did not communicate their own needs.

Most disheartening of all was the number of recruiters who have a clear "why" for doing their job: 2 percent. That's two out of 100. It's shocking! Can you imagine any other profession in which such a huge majority of practitioners are as disconnected from why they're doing their job? What if only 2 percent of doctors found meaning in treating their patients? Or 2 percent of teachers understood why their students should learn the subject material?

It's no wonder so many candidates have such negative interactions with recruiters. That kind of ambivalence seeps into job performance. Recruiters—or any other professional—who are that disconnected from their "why" are distracted, stressed, and careless. They become little more than a cog in a machine, completely divorced from their own power in the talent acquisition dance. Resentment grows—of the hiring manager, the candidate, and the job itself.

Lagging Satisfaction Leads to Lagging Development

It's little surprise, then, that recruiters are often uninterested in developing their EQ. We're not interested in investing in ourselves unless we understand the value of the investment. Most recruiters are simply trying to get through each day. They are juggling the demands of hiring managers and the needs of candidates. They're dealing with ever-changing schedules, communication breakdowns, missed calls, mounting pressures, etc. They are generally overstressed, overstretched, underappreciated, lacking direction and motivation, highly frustrated, and disconnected from their own curiosity and problem-solving abilities. No wonder they often can't find their "why"!

Yet their job is vitally important. Recruiters alter the course of people's lives! They offer a tremendous boon to organizations as well—talent is the biggest driver of success, and a recruiter's job is to get the talent. Recruiting can be exciting and gratifying.

I recommend using the following questions to get a read on your recruitment team's attitudes toward their own development. Whereas the last set of questions was designed to get the recruiter thinking about how to help the company, these are meant to figure out ways for the company to help the recruiter. Your show of good faith that you are invested in the development of your recruiters as both people and professionals will go a long way toward building trust. (That is, as long as you actually follow up on it by working to implement tools to help your recruiters grow.)

To help recruiters find their "why," start by asking:

▶ What is the most stressful part of attracting and retaining talent?
▶ What tools could help you?
▶ What's missing in the organization's approach to attracting and retaining the talent we need?
▶ Why are you a recruiter?
▶ Why do you do what you do?

Your recruiters may not be accustomed to bosses who genuinely care about their personal and professional development. As individuals, we rise to the level of what's expected of us. Your recruitment team is more than just the numbers they produce for the company—but in the past, they may not have been treated as such, and this cold-hearted, bottom-line thinking will be transferred to candidates. Conversely, when you nurture recruiters, you begin a chain reaction of connection. The recruiter extends this sense of connection to candidates, and relationships that have the potential to transform your organization are formed. It all begins with you.

What Recruiters Can Learn from Agile Methodology

Agile methodology is characterized as a lightweight framework by which teams can respond to ever-evolving technology and deliver business value rapidly. Agile methodology is meant to take some of the risk out of experimentation. Developers can respond to changes and fix mistakes in real time, as technology and the business landscape evolve. It's contrasted with the traditional "waterfall" method, a more linear approach in which progress flows in one direction through conception to construction, all the way to deployment and maintenance. In the waterfall method, development flows downward. Agile development is better represented as a circle—deployment of the product occurs before the circle is complete. The product is then tested and reevaluated, and then the circle of development begins again with any necessary adjustments being made.

Yet Agile methodology is not only for technological and product development. Its tenets can be applied to the human-centered business of recruiting, too. Kelly Nestor, head of technical recruiting at CoverMyMeds, used Agile methodologies to rapidly scale her teams and contribute to the company's runaway success.

CoverMyMeds is one of the nation's fastest-growing health-care technology companies. Since joining the organization in 2015, Kelly has tripled the size of the technical teams and built out the product management practice. She's overseen the growth of the work force from 135 employees to more than 800 in four years. With such a rapid rate of growth, Kelly realized that she and her teams simply didn't have time for activities that were not adding value to the organization. "Value over everything" is their motto.

Kelly's teams work closely with software teams that use Agile principles. She was curious: Could incorporating Agile methodologies with her recruitment teams make them happier and more productive at work? The short answer was *yes*!

Kelly spoke of the four core values that compose Agile development:

1. People are more important than processes.
2. Collaboration is more important than negotiation.
3. Solutions are more important than documentation.
4. Responding to change is more important than following a plan.

By making these four values a bedrock of their practices, Kelly and her team experienced amazing results. They could do the most important things fast, focus only on activities that added value, maintain a sustainable working pace, and experience better cohesion as a team. Most important, these four values allowed the team to retain a clear picture of their "why." That's pretty amazing when you consider how frantic and disorganized things can become when a company scales that quickly.

Let's look at each value one by one and see how recruiters might integrate them into their work.

People Are More Important Than Processes

Never lose sight of the human being on the other end of the line, be it a candidate or a hiring manager. Dig into your own humanity. Deploy empathy and continually place yourself in the shoes of the people you're serving. If there's a certain process by which you're required to contact people, follow it, but if you believe the situation calls for another approach, don't be afraid to break with protocol to best serve your clients.

Collaboration Is More Important Than Negotiation

Negotiation implies that two entities are coming to the table with competing desires and only one can win. Collaboration is different—it's when all parties are working together for the greater good. It's not a zero-sum game: Everyone can come out a winner, and the recruiter plays a vital function in making this happen. The goal is for the hiring manager, candidate, and recruiter to walk away from the transaction satisfied, each with their needs met. It's possible!

Solutions Are More Important Than Documentation

What procedures do you currently employ for documenting your interactions with candidates and companies? Are they helping your communication, or slowing it down? In agile development, documentation is meant to be as brief as possible. Communication should be simple but clear, geared toward finding solutions rather than documenting for its own sake.

Responding to Change Is More Important Than Following a Plan

If a recruiter can't adapt to the changing technological landscape, he won't be employed much longer. The AI revolution is transforming the recruiting industry much faster than other sectors of the economy. As new technology continues to be unveiled, recruiters must learn to work with the changes rather than fear them. An emotionally intelligent recruiter who understands his "why" will be able to ride the tide of change brilliantly.

The Emotional Intelligence Factor

From an emotional intelligence lens, it's incumbent on recruiters to enhance their *self-actualization*, one of the pillars of *self-perception*. Self-actualization, as defined by the EQ-i 2.0 system, outlines "the willingness to persistently try to improve oneself and engage in the pursuit of personally relevant and meaningful objectives that lead to a rich and enjoyable life." When recruiters work on self-actualization, their perceptions of themselves—and consequently the importance of their role—increase. The recruiters become connected to their "why" and the tenor of candidate conversations changes. Everything is aligned with a larger purpose.

There's an old story about JFK visiting NASA in 1962. He came across a janitor carrying a broom and asked the man what he was doing.

"Well, Mr. President," said the janitor, "I'm helping put a man on the moon."

The janitor was connected to his *why*. He saw the deeper meaning in what he was doing, even if others might have viewed his role as menial. How might this sense of dignity and larger purpose have carried the janitor throughout his workday?

Once recruiters have this service mindset, their *interpersonal* skills can flourish, especially *empathy*. A recruiter seeking the good of the candidate will engage in empathetic listening and keep the candidate's needs foremost in his mind. Conversations are marked by trust and compassion. Even if the candidate-recruiter-company dance is long and complex and requires great patience, the recruiter doesn't lose sight of the big picture. This way, the recruiter can stay humble and flexible, not taking disappointments too personally or letting success go to her head. It's one way to keep a firm hold on your "why."

This call for recruiters to "dig in" to their humanity becomes more urgent as more of the job is ceded to technology. The recruiting landscape is changing day by day. It's impossible to keep up with the tech. In trying to imagine a way for recruiters to stay abreast of shifting currents while retaining their "why," I believe it's crucial for them to adapt an Agile methodology model, as Kelly Nestor's people did, if they want to position themselves well for growth and scale.

▶ **QUESTIONS FOR REFLECTION** ◀

To understand the impact your recruiters' attitudes are having on your employer brand, ask the right questions. I recommend the ones below. Design a system by which employees can answer anonymously and freely. The answers you receive from your recruitment team will allow you to put your finger on the pulse of their beliefs, feelings, frustrations, etc. You'll then have a clear picture of what recruiters may be transmitting to candidates—either consciously or unconsciously. Most important, it will help you help them identify and honor their "why." Consider asking these questions:

▶ Where do you see your role in the next five years?

▶ How will you get there?

▶ **QUESTIONS FOR REFLECTION** ◀

▶ What do you enjoy the most about your role?

▶ Imagine anything is possible. What would you want to change to make it easier to attract and retain talent within your role?

▶ What do you need to learn to be successful?

▶ What do you want me to know that is important for our success?

▶ How does your function relate to the company's mission?

You need to know where you stand. Knowing your recruiters' honest feelings will give you a clear insight into how candidates are experiencing your company. Remember: You gain nothing when your recruiting team is cautiously polite. Do whatever you can to ensure your team has the freedom to express the full, unvarnished truth and has a firm grasp on why they are doing this work. It's only from that place that you'll be able to grow.

Chapter 6

Elephant: Your Employer Brand Isn't Compelling

When it comes to attracting talent, your employer brand is everything. It's your calling card to would-be unicorns. For companies that aren't Google or Facebook or another giant, a recruiter can provide the first taste of your employer brand. You want them to keep your good reputation intact.

Bryan Chaney, director of employer brand and talent attraction at online recruitment company Indeed, put it this way when he was a guest on the *EI Recruiter* podcast: "Employer brand is all about the story. If we're telling a story that doesn't line up with the actual experience, what might not be a talent attraction problem will turn into an employee engagement and employee retention problem."

Recruiters must tell a good story to get talent through the door. But then the actual employee experience must align with that story. If the two pieces are out of alignment, the new employees will become disenchanted—fast.

A stellar employer brand doesn't happen by accident. Just like everything else, a good employer brand comes from the top. It starts with the CEO consciously thinking about what type of environment he would like to cultivate. People leaders must constantly strive to make sure the culture reflects their highest ideals. What is allowed? What is celebrated? To what does leadership turn a blind eye—and how does that affect people and operations at every level? These are all questions you should be able to answer for potential employees.

A 2018 Stanford study led by Shelley Correll, head of Stanford's Clayman Institute for Gender Research, and Alison Wynn, a postdoctoral researcher at the institute, bore out the importance of developing a strong employer brand to attract top-notch talent. Researchers attended 84 recruiting sessions for top tech firms. These sessions were overwhelmingly led by white men who made frequent references to "geek culture" touchstones such as *Star Trek*. They focused almost exclusively on the technical aspects of coding. The male presenters made frequent attempts to bond with attendees and adopted a loose, off-the-cuff style. This informality allowed for some pretty reprehensible language, including references to pornography and inappropriate sexual behavior. On the few occasions that women did speak, they kept their remarks to generalized statements about company culture. The researchers concluded: "Through gender-imbalanced presenter roles, geek culture references, overt use of gender stereotypes, and other gendered speech and actions, representatives may puncture the pipeline, lessening the interest of women at the point of recruitment into technology careers."

The employer brand seemed to favor a certain type of (white) man. Who knows how many women, after attending these presentations, decided to pack their bags and head into a different industry. That's a tragedy! Warren Buffett famously claimed that one of the reasons he's achieved such success is that he was only competing against half the population. When only half the talent pool is engaged, companies miss out on a wealth of ideas and limit their own potential. These tech companies were only hurting themselves with their blatant displays of "bro culture" in recruiting sessions.

In this chapter, we'll examine how understanding what words you use within your organization influence the way you think and behave with your team and talent you wish to attract. Are you using your words to create a space where all employees feel safe and able to do their best work? We'll see how this dynamic shapes your employer brand—and how that brand affects everything else about your company.

The Words You Use Define You

Words maketh the company. How do you speak to your employees? How do your employees speak to one another? Is language permitted that marginalizes certain groups of people? Is this sort of talk even subtly encouraged? The chauvinistic talk of the tech recruiters in the Stanford study may have driven away talent before they ever had the chance to effect positive change within an organization. Is your company too "dude-centric"? Is one type of political opinion loudly espoused, while others are laughed at or silenced? Is everyone expected to stay beyond the end of the working day (thus sidelining employees with commitments outside of work), and if so, do employees know that?

There's a lot at play here: diversity, culture, and values that drive decisions. Employer branding is complex. There are many different ways an employer brand can be misrepresented, and this can cost you dearly. I heard an amazing story at the annual ERE Media's recruiting conference about an employer brand turnaround and knew I had to speak with its architect, Graeme Johnson. Graeme is the former global head of employer brand and talent acquisition strategy at British Telecommunications (BT). In our conversation on the *EI Recruiter* podcast, he spoke about how telling a truer employer brand story and the words used to communicate can significantly increase profits.

CASE STUDY
How Redefining Your Employer Brand and Its Language Can Change Everything

When Graeme arrived at BT, he'd heard anecdotal accounts of candidates having negative interview experiences, so he set out to measure the impact these bad experiences were having on revenue. He and his team developed a metric by which interviewees could rate their interviewers. Graeme sensed the problem was significant, and he was spot-on. The data revealed that overall, candidates rated their experience as a negative number!

"How many people are we losing by not treating them respectfully?" he asked himself. He next wanted to know the exact cost of having an "in the red" recruiting process, so he and his team crunched the numbers. BT is an enormous brand with approximately 225,000 applicants every year. It's also a subscription broadcasting service. Graeme determined that, as the result of a bad candidate experience, about 10 percent of BT's rejected candidates switched their subscription to a competitor. This amounted to *more than $10 million* in lost revenue annually. The need to strengthen employer brand with different stories became abundantly clear.

Graeme set about doing just that, but he wanted to do it in a way that went beyond the typical "how to improve candidate experience" training provided to HR managers and interviewers. Graeme set out to inspire BT employees—to renew their commitment to and appreciation for the company. This revived sense of purpose and shared identity would then inspire hiring managers to give candidates the best possible experience.

Since he'd arrived at BT from Virgin, Graeme had found the company to have a very low opinion of itself. This self-deprecation belied BT's many accomplishments, from broadcasting the Olympics to managing air traffic control systems to keeping banks in the United Kingdom up and running. Graeme realized that BT needed to do a better job of telling its own stories.

Thus, with the CEO's backing, BT invested in resources to create films that powerfully told the story of its many achievements. The goal was to inspire BT employees and remind them of the greater mission they all served. Then Graeme went after the candidate experience. Because BT invested in telling its own stories well internally, hiring managers approached their work with a renewed sense of pride and a desire to have candidates' experience of BT be similarly positive.

It was a brilliant solution. Graeme's campaign got at the heart of why everyone at BT had a stake in maintaining a positive employer brand.

A Stellar Employer Brand Improves the Candidate Experience

Committed to the goal of improving the candidate experience, Graeme and his team also tested recruitment systems for competitors across the industry by applying for the same job across 25 different organizations. How long did it take? Could candidates apply on their mobile phones? Were there glitches—did the system kick them off?

The team found that length of application time wasn't the only metric by which candidates judged the recruitment system. Candidates did not mind answering questions about themselves even if the questions were somewhat involved. What applicants *did* mind was being asked to reproduce their entire CV. The team discovered that if candidates felt they were repeating themselves unnecessarily, 70 to 80 percent quit filling out the application.

By and large, the industry bar for a satisfactory recruitment process was low. Graeme and his team repeatedly found the application process convoluted and frustrating.

After streamlining BT's application process, Graeme sought to further improve the candidate experience by offering applicants the chance to receive feedback after interviews. The team is currently refining this process, using the same approach taken in marketing: giving candidates information in the way they would most like to receive it.

First, candidates are asked if they would like to receive feedback on their interview. This may take the form of an automated report, which might be positive or negative. The key is that the applicant can *choose* whether to receive it. Graeme's team has found that overall, candidates are open to constructive criticism after interviews. If the applicant knows that feedback is coming, she can prepare herself for a candid performance review and manage her expectations. Even negative feedback is preferable to silence after an interview with a potential employer.

The Emotional Intelligence Factor

From an emotional intelligence lens, offering post-interview feedback is an ingenious way for employers to help candidates with the *stress-management* component of EQ and have a positive effect on the employer brand. In giving candidates the choice of whether to receive feedback, BT is helping them know what to expect during the process and giving them some measure of control. Candidates who feel more in control of their job search have better *stress tolerance* and have a better experience, making the conversations more exploratory and open. They will then share their experience with friends and acquaintances, which positively impacts the employer brand.

I'm a huge fan of Graeme's approach at BT. By strengthening the employer brand internally, Graeme and his team successfully improved the external brand as well. If employer branding truly is all about a story, then it's incumbent on you to tell a good one—and then to ensure that the interactions employees have with one another and with candidates bear that story out.

Any company can do it. You don't have to be a Google or a Facebook to attract unicorns. A bad employer brand is a big elephant. But, as Graeme proved at BT, you can find your way around it to the unicorns standing on the other side.

▶ QUESTIONS FOR REFLECTION ◀

I truly believe that a strong employer brand starts at the top. Graeme could help transform BT's brand because he had the backing of the CEO. Below I invite you to reflect on your leadership's attitude toward your employer brand. Here are some questions to ask yourself, other people leaders, and your recruitment team:

- ▶ If you're the CEO, what are you doing to improve your company's story?
- ▶ How can recruiters pitch that story to candidates?
- ▶ For people leaders at any level, do you see a gap between your employer brand and the candidate experience?
- ▶ If yes, can you identify what changes need to be made?
- ▶ How can you pitch these needed changes to company leadership?

Remember that essentially *every person* in your organization is a recruiter—from the CEO to the actual recruiters and everyone in between. Everyone who works at your company uses language and words to tell its story to the world, whether or not they mean to. Be sure they're telling a good one.

Chapter 7

Elephant: Your Onboarding Process Is Outdated and Impersonal

L et's imagine that your recruiting processes are humming along. Emotionally intelligent recruiters have forged positive relationships with your candidates and told a compelling employer brand story. You've managed to attract your unicorn. Congratulations! You can't wait for her to get started.

Yet something still stands in the way: your onboarding process. The unicorn must listen to a lecture about company history, watch several videos, fill out multiple forms, and work her way through a 3-inch employee handbook binder. *Then* she will be able to properly begin her job. Sound familiar?

So many otherwise great organizations employ this archaic onboarding process, and people accept it as a necessary evil. The hiring manager must cover all bases; forms must be filled out to protect the company in case of liability; the unicorn must learn everything about the company and its greater mission to be effective in her job. Everyone hates this process, yet few companies can imagine a different way forward—they think this is the way things must be done.

An impersonal, grindingly slow onboarding process is an unnecessary elephant keeping your unicorn from reaching her full potential. Think of the excitement you felt when you got the "yes" from your new hire. Think of the excitement the new hire feels. Her enthusiasm and passion are likely what impressed you when you met her. But now, all that energy grinds to a halt.

How might organizations skip the boring parts and make onboarding dynamic—and, dare I say, *fun*? In this chapter, I'll walk you through some ways to bring your onboarding process into this century and make it an asset for your company.

What If Onboarding Were Fun?

A good place to begin is by examining employer brand. In the last chapter, we explored how Graeme Johnson and his team turned BT's employer brand around and created a positive experience for candidates. What story are you telling candidates? Does that story continue to its logical next act once the candidate becomes an employee?

The onboarding process should not deviate from the employer brand. Otherwise, it's a bait-and-switch: "Here are all the great things the company is doing, but not yet! First, you must spend two weeks filling out these mountains of paperwork!" The best onboarding processes immerse the new hire in the organization as soon as possible—not by showing outdated videos, but by quickly engaging the employee in the work.

There's a lot at stake here. Think of it like a marriage—you pull out all the stops to "wow" your unicorn while you're dating. But once you've said "I do," you can't simply treat your unicorn with indifference. If you do that, you lose that spark of passion that drew you together in the first place. Maybe not right away; maybe your unicorn will simply shrug off the frustration of the impersonal process. But do you want to risk it? When you've both got a fresh slate, why force your new hire through all the annoying rigmarole? Your unicorn is raring to go. Putting her through a drawn-out, repetitive onboarding process is like slashing the tires of a brand-new Porsche.

Tips for a Less Painful Onboarding Process

You want to take advantage of your new hire's excitement and work to maximize it. You can do this from day one. If you sense your sluggish onboarding process is an elephant that's preventing your unicorns from launching quickly, here are some tips to make the process more personal—and a lot more enjoyable.

Automate Whatever You Can

Recall in the previous chapter when Graeme and his team were applying with various BT competitors to test their recruiting process. If candidates felt they were having to repeat themselves frequently, 70 to 80 percent dropped out of the application. No one likes to waste time with repetitive data entry. Look into software to streamline your onboarding so that new hires don't have to reenter information they've already given you.

Make It Memorable

Just because you and your unicorn are now in a committed working relationship doesn't mean you should stop treating him with special care. How can you make your new hire's first day memorable? Does your company have a quirky tradition that gets everyone in a loose, silly mood? Are you near an especially cool part of the city to which your new hire and his teammates can take a little field trip? Is there a particularly neat area of the building—music room, yoga studio—that you think your unicorn would like to explore or has expressed an interest in? You only have one first day at a new job. Do what you can to make your unicorn's experience special from day one.

Connect New Hires to the Team Before They Start

Remember finding out who your roommate was going to be before your freshman year at college? Having a connection to someone—even a slight one—can ease anxiety before a new venture begins. Is it possible for you to connect your new hire to their teammates before they start, via social media or some other tool? How can you encourage and incentivize your current team to reach out to the unicorn before his start date? Be creative. If done right (rather than in a way that scares the new hire, the existing team, or both), your efforts can do more than simply make your unicorn feel welcome. If he feels more at home from the beginning, your unicorn is likely to deliver on his potential faster.

Begin Before You Begin

Let's take that previous suggestion a step further. Rather than just connecting a new hire to his team before day one, what *else* can be accomplished before the start date? If you don't yet have technology that allows for a quick and easy, automated "paperwork crunch," can you have your new hire fill out these forms before his first day? Just like a doctor's office asks new patients to fill out forms ahead of their visit, you can have new hires get their paperwork out of the way before beginning work. Other information to consider delivering to the new employee before day one includes:

- ▶ employee directory (with pictures!)
- ▶ orientation plan
- ▶ information about their soon-to-be mentor
- ▶ details about the office location
- ▶ the best spots to grab lunch, coffee, after-work groceries, dry cleaning, etc.

The more information your unicorn has, the more in control of the process he will feel.

Ask for Feedback

Chances are this is not your unicorn's first job. How does your onboarding process compare with his past experiences? Hiring managers should consider developing a system for receiving feedback on the onboarding process, which will serve two purposes. First, candid feedback on what's working and what isn't will help you continually improve. Second, your unicorn will feel like his input is welcome from the very beginning. This will only work, of course, if you are *actually* interested in the new hire's feedback and communicate this openly. When a new employee (or any member of your team) gives you her opinion, you must thank her for her truthfulness. Most people are scared to give criticism, no one more so than a brand-new employee. Yet the faster you can get to a place of honest sharing with your new hire, the more quickly you'll be able to drive toward goals together. (We'll talk more about giving and receiving feedback in Chapter 8.)

Embed Coaching in Your Onboarding

I once coached a new hire at a large tech company who had worked there for *months* without meeting with the hiring manager. Everyone was plowing ahead with the best intentions, attempting to do their work without actually having formed relationships (the way it often works for remote offices). In cases like these, it's helpful to have a coach or another third party say, "Everybody STOP!" I was able to fill this role, as I was unattached to the emotional currents and office politics of this particular workplace. In that instance, I served a simple function: merely bringing everyone (the chief people officer, the CEO, the new hire) together to ensure that all parties were on the same page. I was the connecter, reminding the chief people officer that the new hire was an actual *person*! It's easy to forget this in remote work scenarios. Yet when we disconnect from the humanity of our colleagues, we create a breeding ground for resentments. Without this official "coming together" time, that hiring manager might have simply viewed my client as a number on a spreadsheet ("How much are we spending on this person, anyway? Is he really worth it?") rather than as a teammate whose personal success is crucial to the larger success of the company.

Everyone needs a coach in their first 100 days, although this will look different depending on your level in the company. CEOs need an executive coach. For lower-level employees, a mentor is a must. The key is for all parties—the new hire, the mentor/coach, and the boss—to come together and determine what metrics they are going to hold themselves to. What will success in the first 100 days look like? How will it be measured? In what areas does the new hire (whatever her level) need to grow, and how can a coach help her get where she needs to be? Then regularly set aside some time—at least once a week—so that the new hire can have sessions with her coach or mentor.

Can you imagine how connected and supported your unicorn would feel with this system as part of the onboarding process? With seasoned professionals, there can often be a dangerous assumption that we've all done this before. *The new hire will be fine on her own and will reach out if she really needs help.* The "bigger" the job, the less importance is given to onboarding. But you can't skip this crucial step. Employees who have strong relationships at work are more likely to stay and achieve their potential. The best way to help your unicorn feel supported is by showing her from day one that her team has her back.

Best Practices for Onboarding

At FORWARD, we provide 100 days of coaching for every candidate we place. No one can opt out of this; it's a nonnegotiable part of our process. Why am I so adamant about it? Because getting hired is just the beginning. I am invested in making sure that all the candidates we place succeed; that means providing them the support they need as they begin their new roles so we can help set them up to achieve their potential.

Here's a peek into our process:

1. On day four of a new hire's first week in his position, we gather all the people invested in his success. A coach facilitates by leading the group through the following questions:
   - ▶ How is everything going on Day 4?
   - ▶ What's the vision for the role?
   - ▶ Where is the company going?
   - ▶ What are the opportunities?
   - ▶ What are the challenges?
   - ▶ Where do you all want to be in 30/60/90 days?

2. We hold mandatory, weekly one-hour remote coaching sessions with the new hire. In these sessions, we discuss wins from the previous week as well as possible solutions to any challenges that emerge.

3. We perform an EQ-i 2.0 assessment and debrief within the first two weeks. This allows us to discover and examine the new hire's go-to behaviors and emotional intelligence growth areas with the goal of identifying new behaviors that would enhance his success.

4. At the end of the first 100 days, we hold a 360-degree review with the same stakeholders who gathered on day four. The self-reflection exercise below helps everyone identify their role over the past 100 days and directs the new hire on ways to improve and evolve over the next six months. We ask the following questions:
   ▶ What has <name> achieved in the past 100 days?
   ▶ Can you describe an area where <name> can improve?
   ▶ What three areas/attributes do you like about <name> in the role of <title>?
   ▶ How can you see <name> progressing in the next six months?
   ▶ Is there anything else you'd like to share?

As coach, I refer back to the original deck I co-created with the new hire and stakeholders during the first kickoff meeting, and we cross-check to determine how well all parties met the objectives laid out at our day four meeting.

The Emotional Intelligence Factor

A strong onboarding process puts your new hire's *interpersonal relationships* (the third component of emotional intelligence) foremost. For the well-being of your new hire, it's imperative she connects to her peers. *New York Times* bestselling author Shawn Achor, along with a team of experts, conducted a study of loneliness in the work force, the findings of which were documented in the *Harvard Business Review* in 2018. He and his team surveyed more than 1,600 employees to find who was most at risk of feeling lonely. They found that lawyers were the loneliest workers, followed by engineers and those in the science fields. There was a 10-percent decrease in loneliness for people making more than $80,000 a year. Geographic location and length of time spent working with one organization had little bearing on loneliness. Government workers were lonelier than people in the private sector. Singles were lonelier than married people. Troublingly, LGBTQ people reported high degrees of loneliness and lower levels of workplace support.

How does this impact you? Why does it matter? As a people leader who wants to lead teams of satisfied, healthy contributors to your organization's growth, you need to be on the lookout for signs that your workers feel isolated. We spend an enormous portion of our lives at work. It's impossible to divorce the mental and social well-being of a teammate from her job performance. If your new hire hits several indicators that suggest she would be prone to loneliness, are there any extra efforts you could take to make sure she feels supported?

At the end of the day, it is about achieving your benchmarks. You want to retain your unicorns for the value they'll bring to your organization. It is best, then, to ensure that they feel supported and part of the larger team from the very beginning. If you're aware that your impersonal onboarding process is an elephant, I invite you to evaluate it in light of this question: Is this process increasing or decreasing the level of connection my new hire feels to her colleagues? If the answer is "decreasing," how can you tweak your onboarding to make it more human? Ask the question, and then listen to whatever feedback comes to you through various channels: your own intuition, long-standing employees, and new hires alike. Onboarding doesn't *have* to suck; with some adjustments, you may even discover you can make it fun.

▸ QUESTIONS FOR REFLECTION ◂

Now it's time to reflect on your onboarding practices. Don't rely solely on your own estimation—ask your employees, both brand-new hires and those who have been with the company for several years. Those closest to the onboarding process have a wealth of knowledge for you to tap. See what they say about these questions:

▶ QUESTIONS FOR REFLECTION ◀

- ▶ What was the most memorable part of onboarding?

- ▶ Were you partnered with a mentor? How was this relationship for you?

- ▶ Was onboarding too fast? Too slow? Tedious? Overwhelming?

- ▶ What's one thing the company could have done to make the process better?

That last question is key. It provides data you can act on. It's also a chance for newer employees to own their leadership abilities: When they see their feedback implemented in the onboarding process for new employees, they will gain a tangible sense of how they are contributing to the greater good of the organization.

Chapter 8

Elephant: You Don't Know How to Give and Receive Effective Feedback

I like a turkey and cranberry sandwich. A BLT. A British Marks & Spencer's prawn mayonnaise on granary bread. A real butter and marmite sandwich on a crusty white loaf. What I *hate* is a feedback sandwich.

We all know how it goes. Say something nice, then say something critical, then say something nice again to round it out. It's a worn-out formula with a good intention behind it. Bosses are, in general, petrified of saying anything negative to their employees, especially someone they like and care about. Thus, the feedback sandwich was invented so bosses could couch the "negative"—which is most likely the point of the entire interaction—between two banal "positives."

But employees can see right through it. If you ask to have a private conversation with someone on your team, chances are his antenna is all the way up. If you have feedback for him that will help him execute his role better, he'll be relieved, not hurt.

In this chapter, we'll talk about how to "get right to it" when giving feedback and how to do it in a way that makes you vulnerable and builds trust with your team members. The goal is honesty that leads to improved relationships and better work. For feedback to be effective, it must flow both ways between you and your direct report.

Why the Feedback Sandwich Is Hard to Swallow

Remember: Your employees are *smart*. If something is wrong on the team or with their own performance, they know it. The longer you let the issue go on without addressing it, the more uncomfortable everyone feels. An inability to directly address problems when they arise sows confusion. Team members may think, "Am I crazy? Can't everyone see what a drag on the team Person X is?" Or, "My boss doesn't seem to realize I'm having a problem with this. Is she really that out of it?" Or, "Person Y is bringing our team down and the boss is turning a blind eye—she must like him more." Suspicions and resentments form.

Still, most of us would rather eat our own hair than confront others. This reluctance stems from lots of different reasons. We're afraid our team members will turn on us. We anticipate employees' emotional reactions and want to prevent them from becoming sad or frustrated. For women, gender dynamics can play a role: The quest to be "likable" can lead us to avoid difficult conversations. So feedback avoidance becomes the invisible elephant in the room. When struggling teammates are not confronted directly, your unicorns end up picking up the slack, and eventually they will burn out. If it's your unicorn who's struggling, your discomfort with providing feedback bars you from having candid conversations about his performance, and ultimately better positioning him to serve your organization.

Of course, feedback doesn't have to be negative. Refraining from giving positive feedback is just as deadly. We've all heard the adage "praise in public, criticize in private," but that's not necessarily true. Some of your team members might rather have a tooth pulled than be acknowledged publicly, no matter how warm the accolade. You have to know them as individuals. Taking the time to learn what motivates your direct reports will allow you to give feedback—both positive and negative—in the way they are most likely to hear it.

But first, you must establish trust.

Trust: The First Building Block of Effective Feedback

Your direct reports have to know you care about them as individuals. Trust is key—and trust takes time. It is built through small daily interactions. Taking the time to get to know your employees personally—asking about their lives and being sincerely interested in the answers—is more than just chitchat. These conversations are how relationships are built. They are not a distraction from your work. These conversations are actually *part of your job* as a people leader.

If employees don't sense that you care for them as people, your feedback is not going to be well-received. Simply put, you run the risk of sounding like a total jerk. As Kim Scott details in her 2017 book *Radical Candor*, employees would rather work for a jerk who gets results than for a boss who is "too nice." "Too nice" means that important issues are not being confronted, there are lots of areas of slack, and some team members are shouldering more than their share.

But these two options present a false dichotomy. As a people leader, you don't have to choose between being a pushover who fails to deliver or a bully who gets results. You can care personally and challenge your team in a way that inspires and motivates them to do their best work.

How to Gain Integrity When Giving Feedback

Here's a secret: You will have a lot more integrity when offering feedback if your team sees you *receiving* feedback. The best people leaders work hard to dissolve the hierarchical boundaries that prevent team members lower on the ladder from speaking out when they see a problem higher up. They put systems in place by which any person, no matter his rank, can "pull the lever," so to speak, and stop the chain of production. People leaders within these organizations establish a sense of shared responsibility for all aspects of the company's success. Whatever a person's rank, she should be able to speak out if there's a problem; the best leaders can set aside their egos and listen to legitimate criticism, no matter who it's coming from.

Establishing this kind of culture is *hard*. But to quote Tom Hanks in *A League of Their Own*: "It's supposed to be hard. If it wasn't hard, everyone would do it. The hard is what makes it great." Not everyone is up for creating a candid company culture. Not every people leader is committed to giving and receiving truthful, sometimes tough feedback from *everyone*. But people leaders who want to lead great teams and great organizations are.

Yet when you're the boss, it's rare to find lower-level employees who will speak their minds candidly. There's a strange dynamic shift when you become a manager. Suddenly, team members with whom you've enjoyed open, frank relationships in the past clam up. Everyone wants to be on their best behavior around you. Something in our brains is so afraid of challenging authority that we'll do almost anything to convince ourselves that we don't need to speak up when there's a problem. "I guess it's not all *that* bad." "It's probably just me—I need to find a way to deal with it." Yet true growth only comes when people are free to speak their minds and confront problems.

Why It's So Hard for Your Direct Reports to Give You Feedback

I've encountered this uncomfortable dynamic in my own work when direct reports left unexpectedly—at least, it was unexpected to *me*. This played out memorably with two former employees—we'll call them Ben and Rebecca. Rebecca was not entirely happy with her job description at FORWARD. I would talk about benchmarks we needed to meet, and Rebecca would say, "I'm not comfortable doing that." My inner response was: *What do you mean? It's part of your job!* Yet Rebecca never felt she could speak freely about the parts of her job that were a bad fit. I suspect she may have disliked the payment structure: commissions on top of a base salary, rather than a salary with bonuses based on company performance. I wish she had felt secure enough to talk to me about it and find a solution. What could I have done to establish a more trusting environment in which she felt free to share her concerns? Had I done that, I believe I could have helped Rebecca lean into the aspects of the job that sparked her interests and used her talents. She might still have left, but we would have had more of a sense of closure. And Rebecca would have gone into her next position with a more complete knowledge of her wants and needs and the language to articulate those desires more clearly.

Similarly, I longed to speak candidly with Ben, another direct report at FORWARD. I could tell he was not bringing his whole self to work, and I wanted to know why. I pried: "What's going on? You're drifting off. I can tell you're not really into it." I wanted to help him succeed; that's my job. But Ben didn't feel he could tell me what was wrong *because* I was the boss. In my mind, I was working hard to establish a trusting working relationship. In Ben's mind, speaking openly about his mistakes and struggles would be like telling on himself to the teacher. We were at an impasse. When we parted ways soon thereafter, I was left with a feeling of regret for all the conversations we'd never had.

So how can you as a people leader encourage candor from your direct reports? You have to continually ask for feedback on *yourself* and heap praise on the team members who actually give it. Acknowledge openly that you have struggles and need to course correct, too. If your direct reports don't give you feedback when you ask for it, wait. Sit in silence for an uncomfortably long time. Then ask again. They'll eventually say something, just to get out of the room! When they do, be *exuberant* in your gratitude. Your direct reports will get the picture: When you ask for feedback, you really mean it. They need to know you won't bite their heads off for speaking the truth.

We mentioned earlier that a boss should criticize in private and praise in public. When *you're* the one being criticized, though, that adage is flipped on its head. You *have* to receive public criticism from your direct reports. They must see you receiving criticism if it is to become a regular feature of your work culture. And once the feedback has been given, you must thank the person bold enough to speak his mind to the boss.

Does this mean you have to act on the criticism? No. You're allowed to think the feedback is off-base or misguided. But you should know if the person who spoke out did so in good faith. If this is the case, you must thank him in public. You can have your own reaction later in private. Whether or not the feedback leads to changes in your team or the larger organization, honor the person who offered his opinion by sitting with whatever he has said. Never react in the moment; don't shut down someone speaking truthfully by telling him how he is mistaken or why his suggestion will never work. Say "thank you"—again and again, so that other direct reports will feel encouraged to speak up, too—and then give the suggestion space so that you can, in time, give a thoughtful response.

Feedback Can (and Should) Be Collaborative

I love Pixar cofounder Ed Catmull's description of their Braintrust meetings in his 2014 book *Creativity, Inc.* In these meetings, directors come together with other colleagues who have deep experience in storytelling—writers, story editors, etc.—to workshop their films. The purpose of these meetings is to see what's working and what isn't as the other storytellers offer feedback in a judgment-free zone.

In this collaborative environment, storytellers set aside their egos and listen to candid feedback from top minds who have a vested interest in their success. The directors *know* the product needs work, so the purpose of these meetings is to take the movie "from suck to not-suck." Ed, a former academic, brought the concept of peer review with him to Pixar. The candid environment he helped create is one of the reasons Pixar consistently delivers top-notch entertainment.

Meetings run this way are a brilliant way to get at the heart of a problem. Receiving candid feedback from others who value your success is crucial to your development. It's the process by which artists refine their vision and create masterworks. Every novel on the shelves has been read by many other people who helped the author shape the narrative into something more satisfying. No television show emerged fully formed; it endured a process of narrowing the creator's vision and homing in on the elements that really make it click. Artists understand the value of candid feedback, no matter where it comes from. Likewise, people leaders who want to create strong and healthy teams need to foster ways of delivering and receiving feedback all the time.

I'm not talking about performance reviews. There is plenty of debate concerning how often performance reviews should happen or even whether they should be done away with altogether. I won't get into that, but I will say that whatever you tell your direct reports in their performance review should be no surprise. Your ongoing dialogue with your team members should be conducted so that they are aware of concerns with their performance in *real time*. If you hold off on negative feedback until the performance review, your direct report will feel sucker-punched. You'll make yourself sick with dread thinking, "Now I really have to tell her. Can't avoid this conversation any longer." Most important, you will have wasted valuable time in which the two of you could have faced the problem head-on and come up with a solution.

CASE STUDY
How Creating a "Self-User Manual" Can Position Your Teams for Success

Jay Desai is the cofounder and CEO of the health-care startup PatientPing. As of this writing, the company has 100 employees, with seven reporting directly to Jay. Leading a startup is a high-pressure gig. There are innumerable opportunities for miscommunications, unclear expectations, and general confusion. That's why Jay decided to get ahead of those issues with a brilliant solution: a user manual for *himself*. In it, he details how he gives feedback and how he would like team members to communicate with him. He spoke with me about the method behind the manual.

"As a younger executive, I struggled with management in the early days," Jay told me. When there were communication troubles, he said, pinning down the source was difficult. *Is it you? Is it me?* "I felt like I was doing wrong by my reports," said Jay. "I thought, 'Why is this so hard?'"

In an attempt to bypass those problems, he created his self-user manual. It's a guide for his direct reports so they understand from the start of the working relationship what to expect from Jay as a boss. The guide is detailed, covering everything from preferred methods of communication and how to contact him for the most urgent matters to issues like personal space (Jay asks them to tell him if he is violating team members' space).

Jay calls creating and sharing his user guide an "act of empathy." The goal is to set radically clear expectations from the beginning: to build trust with his direct reports and signify that he is committed to growth, both theirs and his own. It's a brilliant way to establish that communication and feedback will flow both ways in the boss-employee relationship.

Jay introduces his user guide in interviews. Some candidates are *thrilled* that their prospective boss has laid out his expectations, habits, quirks, etc. so plainly and taken the guesswork out of the relationship. Others are turned off by it: They find the guide overwhelming and don't jibe with Jay's working style. Either reaction is invaluable: For candidates who become hires, he has already begun to build a level of trust before their first onboarding day. And candidates who don't continue know that the job wouldn't be a good fit and can cut their losses with no hard feelings on either side. Jay's honesty brings forth their own.

Jay's user guide is a fabulous example of a boss deploying openness and vulnerability. Everyone wants to be authentic and vulnerable these days, but few know how to do it. Jay told me that his team were not initially onboard when he first created it. It is unusual for a CEO to be so transparent and forthcoming about his own flaws. Yet Jay has gained immeasurable value from his strategic use of candor.

"What people want from their leaders is honesty and authenticity," he said. "You need to be really comfortable in your own skin. Know who you are, love who you are. Then you can be there for your employees." Jay found that by "putting it all out there"—yet still acknowledging workplace dynamics and roles—he could build trust quickly. And trust is the first building block of effective feedback. "I talk a lot about trust with our employees," said Jay. "Trust is a superpower. Trust can be an elephant in the room. Trust comes through feeling like you're being your authentic self."

The result for his teams? Liberation. According to Jay, his direct reports can now manage his expectations—*not* his personality. When Jay communicates in a way that could be interpreted as blunt, his direct reports understand the intent behind the request, and friction is minimized. In one-on-ones, employees will tell him, "I went back and I read the user guide, and I think that *this* may be a better way to approach XYZ." Jay has found that his user guide not only helps him communicate with direct reports but also enables direct reports to communicate better with one another. In turn, many of his direct reports have created their own user manuals. (Want to create one for yourself? Visit https://managerreadme.com/, where you'll find a template for your own user guide.)

Jay said that back before he was a CEO, he and his colleagues would often gripe about the boss. But it's difficult to complain about the boss when the boss has already put the "complainable" stuff out there. Jay said, "I've owned the less desirable parts of myself."

If that's not an example of an emotionally intelligent leader, I don't know what is.

The Emotional Intelligence Factor

If you've served too many foul "feedback sandwiches," bringing awareness to the problem is the first step. Enhancing your EQ, particularly the *self-expression* component, is crucial for people leaders who want to get better at giving feedback. *Self-expression* is made up of three subcategories. The first is *emotional expression*. People leaders who wish to express their emotions well must first be able to acknowledge them. "I'm feeling XYZ" (frustrated, anxious, sad, etc.). From this point of awareness, they can relate to others without being ruled by their predominating feelings or transmitting negative emotion.

The second component is *assertiveness*: communicating your feelings, thoughts, and beliefs openly in an inoffensive, nondestructive manner. If your employees know that you care for the person you're speaking with, you'll be poised to deliver direct feedback without causing offense. You won't need to backpedal and mitigate your feedback with false assurances and meaningless praise. Remember: Employees would rather work for an efficient jerk than a pushover nice guy. Cushioning your criticism too much will only cause confusion. But you don't have to choose—employees who know that you can demonstrate your care and regularly see *you*, the boss, receiving and implementing feedback are more likely to take your criticism in good faith and work to improve.

The final component of *self-expression* is *independence*: the ability to be self-directed and free of emotional dependency on others. You care about your direct reports. You don't want them to be pained by what you have to say. Yet when you try to manage their emotional response to criticism, you're setting yourself up for a world of hurt. Learning to resist the urge to manage other people's emotions for them can be a long process. But remember: *You're not doing your direct reports any favors* by being "too nice." In fact, failing to be assertive when delivering criticism isn't really about your direct reports at all—it's about you.

We all want to be liked. If you suffer from a "disease to please," the desire to be liked can be so intense it's almost painful. Yet the journey of becoming emotionally intelligent involves taking responsibility for your emotions and desires—including the desire to be liked—and seeing how they are helping or harming you and those around you. Rather than helping your direct reports, your disease to please could actually be harming them. Failing to communicate issues clearly will leave your employees confused. But that doesn't give you an excuse to act like a jerk. If you can't maintain your emotional independence by realizing that you are responsible for your emotional reactions and no one else's, you will muddle interactions—and ultimately cripple your team.

The ability to receive and implement candid feedback is how we grow. The ability to *give* candid feedback is necessary for any boss who wants her team to flourish. If feedback avoidance is an elephant for you, take heart. This stuff can be learned. With emotional intelligence, you can navigate the sometimes difficult process of giving and receiving feedback until it becomes second nature.

▶ QUESTIONS FOR REFLECTION ◀

How does feedback flow in your organization? Below are some questions for you to consider:

- ▶ Do you as a boss regularly ask for feedback from your direct reports?
- ▶ Do they actually give it?
- ▶ If not, how could you empower your direct reports to be candid with you?
- ▶ What is one change you've made in how you work based on feedback you've received?

Regarding the last question: If you can't think of any changes you've made in your behavior based on feedback you've received, you've got a problem. For whatever reason, you have a

> ► **QUESTIONS FOR REFLECTION** ◄

hard time asking for feedback, hearing feedback, acting on feedback—or all of the above. But awareness of the problem is the first step toward finding a solution. Recognize that it *is* possible to implement thoughtful feedback while still standing on your integrity. That's how you get better, and that's what we're after.

Chapter 9

Elephant: Your Employees Are Disengaged

L et's imagine that your unicorn has moved through the recruiting and onboarding processes and is now a stellar member of your team. Hurray! He is delivering on his potential and leading the organization to new levels. Now the question becomes: How do you keep him from jumping ship?

As a people leader, you have to know what motivates your direct reports. We spend an enormous amount of time at work. We want our work to be meaningful, to see the connection between the job that pays our bills and our larger hopes and dreams. Your job as a people leader is to help make this happen for your direct reports. When employees feel disconnected from their larger selves, they become disengaged from their work, too.

This is especially true for younger generations, the Millennials and Gen Z'ers. You won't get any generation-bashing from me. I admire how our younger cohorts, especially Millennials, feel so committed to effecting positive change in the world. Millennials as a group eschew compartmentalization. According to a 2010 Pew Research study, they desire work that engages all of themselves; they want to feel committed to a higher purpose. Here I run the risk of stereotyping, but these trends have been widely reported on. I also want to avoid labeling all younger workers as Millennials. I recognize that the oldest members of this generation are approaching 40. For the purposes of this discussion however, I'll address Millennials specifically, as members of Gen Z were born after 1995, so it is difficult to measure their impact on the work force at this point.

Millennials have not grown up with a "silo mentality." They don't expect to be one person at work, another at home, and a third with their friends. Millennials are aware of the danger to which this kind of thinking can lead. Many came of age with the Great Recession. They saw up close how greed, unchecked and disconnected from the lives of real people, tanked the housing market and wrecked the economy. This crisis was the backdrop against which many younger people entered the work force. For many of them, the question, "Is it good for business?" may not be enough. The bigger question is: "Is it good for *people*?"

No matter the age of your work force, team members will do their best work when they are connected to the larger picture of how they are making a positive contribution to the world. Employee engagement starts with one all-important question: "Why?"

The Company "Why" Drives Employee Engagement

As you read in Chapter 5, if your business is ultimately going to add value and meaning to lives, employees have to be connected to their "why." But it's not just the employees' "why" that matters—the company one matters as well because that helps drive employee engagement on a larger scale. If you want to avoid employee disengagement, you have to be able to identify your company's "why" and connect it to that of your teams. Do you communicate the core values of your company from day one? Does your "why" drive all your decisions? Working to make sure your team members feel connected to the larger "why" is one way to keep them engaged.

Yvon Chouinard is a great example of a leader connected to his "why." Chouinard is the founder of Patagonia and a passionate nature lover. Patagonia is a $750 million company; yet in making decisions, company leadership has remained committed to a love of the earth rather than the pursuit of fast profits. Early on, Patagonia stopped making the metal spikes for climbing, called pitons, that were its first product because of the damage they caused to rock faces. Chouinard later took an even bigger risk by switching to all-organic cotton for clothing fabric. Today, Patagonia remains committed to conservation and has lobbied against moves by the Trump administration to shrink national parks and monuments.

It pays to get crystal clear about your values, mission, and vision early on. These values drive decisions and shape your employer brand. That way, you attract employees who are already aligned with what you want to do in the world. Your company draws to itself unicorns who are ready to jump into the work with both feet.

That's the work that takes place before the work: gaining clarity on mission and values (the company "why") and then strengthening employer brand so that top-notch employees are drawn to you. But once you have your team of unicorns, you must work to make sure they stay engaged.

See the Whole Person

This part of the work begins with recognizing a simple fact: Your unicorns are so much more than the job they've been hired for. This is another way of saying that people leaders need to see the whole person, not just the job description. To care personally about your direct reports, you must allow them to be who they are—not just what the role demands of them.

Managers fall into a trap when they look at an employee's resume and expect him to replicate past successes beat for beat. "I see what you did with company XYZ—now do that exact same thing for us!" This ignores the context in which the unicorn achieved his past success. What was his team like there? Will he be similarly supported in your organization? Was he given the freedom to innovate and think outside the box at his past company, and will he have that freedom here? Moreover, this impulse ignores the person. Sure, the unicorn accomplished a lot in his role at his previous company. But how has he evolved since then? Is the position you're considering him for in line with his career growth? Or could his talents best be utilized in another capacity within the organization? Most important, *what does he want*?

This pigeonhole thinking played out in my own life earlier in my career. I'd enjoyed success as the UK PR manager at Sony for the PlayStation launch. I felt pride in the accomplishment and exhilaration as PlayStation went on to crush the competition. But then I wanted to do something else. The launch was incredibly exciting, but I didn't want to keep "babysitting" launches. I was drawn to the more people-centered work of human resources rather than the branding and marketing work of PR. However, back then, HR was more about writing job descriptions than coaching and equipping people for leadership. My "dream job" didn't yet exist. I would have to forge my own path.

Yet people had a very hard time accepting it. Years after the PlayStation launch, I was still being pigeonholed as a PR executive. It was a confusing time for me. I'd thrown myself into PR and become very passionate about the job. No wonder others had me pegged in the role. I had to work hard to change my own narrative and create a career that merged my strengths and passions.

It took time for me to claim all my different passions—to become, as author Jeff Haden puts it, an "and" person. I was hugely influenced by his 2018 book *The Motivation Myth*. In it, Haden speaks of the need to claim all our different interests. Over the past 30 years, the way we work has changed, but the way we talk about work has not. We still speak to college students about finding their passion: the one career path that will fulfill them intellectually, emotionally, and financially. Yet this does not reflect a true work experience—especially now, when most of us have four or five (or more) different careers over the course of our lifetimes. Nor does it reflect a true *life* experience.

No one has just one interest. When I was trying to break out of my PR executive mold, I wished desperately that hiring managers would understand that. Your direct reports, too, are multifaceted people with many passions. A surefire path to employee disengagement is to stifle their interests in tasks that fall outside their job descriptions. "You can't do that—that's a marketing thing." Or, "We don't need you to lead that training. That's what we have a training department for." Effective people leaders see their employees as varied, complex individuals. They expect team members to do their jobs, but they're always interested in their employees' unique interests and passions, and they strive to draw these out within the context of their assigned tasks.

What Seeing the Whole Person Looks Like in the Workplace

Google famously honors the many talents and interests of its employees by allowing Googlers 20 percent of their work time—one whole day a week—for work-related passion projects. Good leaders recognize that if our brains get too accustomed to any one task, we get bored. We need to take on new challenges and explore new interests so that we're ready to face whatever problems may come our way. How can you facilitate this type of dynamism on your team?

Once again, the key is to care personally. You have to know your teammates and know what motivates them. This requires people leaders to really dig in and have nonthreatening but in-depth conversations. How many times have you sat down to have an honest discussion with your direct reports and ended up with something like this?

You: "Where do you see yourself in five years?"

Your direct report: "I'd like to be where you are, doing exactly what you're doing."

This may be gratifying to your ego, but you can safely assume it's false. What *really* gets your direct reports excited? Is it the prospect of holing up with a complex engineering problem? Or do they come alive at the thought of managing others? Even if you discover that your unicorn's secret passion lies completely outside his job description—let's say he ultimately wants to open a school for children in a developing country—you can still use that information by connecting it to the work he's doing for your organization. If he wants to open a school, he'll need experience overseeing administrative issues, so when those opportunities arise, seize them. Tell your unicorn, "I thought this role would be a good fit because of your wish to strengthen your administrative abilities." He will likely be gratified and motivated to do a stellar job because you cared enough to remember his interests and let him shepherd his own growth and because he can see how the work he's doing now can help get him where he ultimately wants to be. (If you're unsure how to structure conversations like these, I've included a resource list of questions for you at the end of this chapter.)

Put Yourself in Your Direct Reports' Shoes

I once coached someone—we'll call him Anthony—during his first 100 days on a job who was enthusiastic and ready to jump in until, all of a sudden, he wasn't. He completely ghosted me. It seemed so out of character, so I was determined to find out what was going on.

I'd worked with Anthony's boss (let's call him Henry) the previous year. "What's going on with Anthony?' I asked. "He was so excited!"

"It's unfortunate," said Henry. "Anthony's attitude is really deteriorating."

"Why?"

"I'm not sure," he said. But as Henry went on, he told me about *three* major earthquakes Anthony had endured within his first 100 days. The project for which he had been hired had been canceled; a whole slew of people had been laid off, and the person who'd hired Anthony had left to work for a competitor.

I felt like grabbing the nearest megaphone and shouting into my phone, "No wonder his attitude is deteriorating!" But I kept calm. "Don't you think all these significant changes in the organization are why Anthony's attitude is 'deteriorating,' as you say?" I asked. "In fact, he is probably looking for a different job as we speak." Henry was taken aback. *I* was surprised by *his* surprise. Could he not understand how conflicted and desolate Anthony probably felt? When I contacted Anthony and told him I knew about the situation and understood why he was reluctant to get in touch, he sounded relieved. He spoke candidly about how he felt. He was angry and upset. He was just trying to keep his head down and figure out what his role was since it seemed to change by the day. Anthony said he didn't have the mental or emotional energy for coaching at the moment. I was thankful for his candor and told him I completely understood.

As Anthony's coach, I was able to bring perspective to both Anthony and Henry. Anthony was in the weeds, while Henry was so focused on his own issues that he hadn't considered how the company shake-ups had deeply affected his brand-new hire. Anthony had very, very good reasons for disengaging with me. His work landscape suddenly looked completely different from the one he'd been hired into. He felt as if he did not have the backing of company leadership—an all-too-common problem for employees in "fixed mindset" companies (more on that in the next section).

Anthony was lacking empathy from his bosses. No one was checking in with him on a human-to-human level, so of course, he became disillusioned, stressed, and disengaged. If you as a people leader sense that one of your direct reports has withdrawn, stop and place yourself in his shoes. See the situation from a new perspective, and then make a genuine connection with the team member and work together toward a solution. Near disaster was averted when Henry was able to understand how disorienting a time it must have been for Anthony, and the relationship, communications, and engagement improved.

Drive Engagement with a Growth Mindset

Does your company have a growth mindset or a fixed mindset? Carol Dweck, a psychology professor at Stanford University, has studied and written extensively on how growing and constantly improving is adopting a growth mindset for success. Fixed-mindset companies, on the other hand, tend to reward a select few who perform in a traditional way with promotions and raises. Employees who are *not* perceived as premier leaders at these fixed-mindset companies are more afraid of taking risks and feel that management does not have their backs. They display less commitment than workers at growth-mindset companies and are more likely to keep secrets and cheat to get ahead.

Organizations with a growth mindset view talent differently. Managers tend to speak more positively about their direct reports. Many are more likely to say that their employees have management potential. At these companies, collaboration is the norm. It's expected that employees across the organization, whatever their level, will look for out-of-the-box solutions and seek to grow and develop new skillsets while at the company. Dweck's research indicates that adopting a growth mindset takes a lot of work, but it can be done if the CEO is committed to developing employees. Growth-mindset companies frequently hire from within; hiring managers are interested in potential and reward candidates who display a passion for learning.

Though research is not yet conclusive on which model is more profitable, I'm heavily in favor of the growth mindset as it relates to employee engagement. People leaders who invest in their employees' learning and development create an exciting environment to work in. That's something you don't find everywhere else, which helps with employee retention. Why would a unicorn leave a job in which her boss truly cares about her, her mind is engaged, and she is developing a diverse set of useful skills?

We are all so much more than the job we've been hired for. We want a workplace that allows us to bring our whole selves to work and that understands we have needs and lives outside the office. No one takes a job without careful consideration of how it will affect every other area of life: "This job will provide great health benefits for my child with special needs," or, "Working through the weekend is not expected here, so I can take more hiking trips," or, "This job has great parental leave in case I decide to start a family." You don't need to know every detail of your direct reports' personal lives. But you *do* need to invest time in getting to know your team and creating a safe space in which they can feel supported when they come to you with pressing personal matters.

For example, how will you respond if a direct report comes to you with a cancer diagnosis? If a team member is on leave, do you have a system in place to check up on her throughout her absence? If a direct report confides he is considering starting a family, is he aware of the company benefits and guidelines for parental leave? Being a people leader means caring about the *whole* employee. It also means being open about your own life: "I'm having a rough time because the baby was up screaming between midnight and 4 A.M., so forgive me if I'm a little unfocused today." A simple admission like this requires a certain amount of vulnerability and reminds your direct reports that you're a human being, too. All this is part and parcel of the growth mindset and helps you achieve greater levels of employee engagement.

The Emotional Intelligence Factor

Engaged employees have higher levels of *self-perception* (the first component of emotional intelligence). They are working toward *self-actualization* (a subcategory of *self-perception*) by pursuing things they find meaningful and improving and broadening their skill sets. An emotionally intelligent boss can model *emotional self-awareness*, which also falls under the umbrella of *self-perception*. A boss with high EQ levels acknowledges her emotions and takes responsibility for them, thus creating an environment in which it is safe for team members to do the same. Negative emotions are not given free rein. Rather, when there is stress or frustration—or, on the flip side, joy and excitement—both boss and direct reports have the freedom to express those feelings without letting them interfere with the work at hand.

Genuinely caring about your direct reports (and making sure *they know* you truly care) is one of the most important things you do as a people leader. Allowing people space to be their whole selves will mean so much more than any raise or promotion ever could. Think of someone in your own life who really knows you and has been committed to your growth as a person. How devoted are you to them, even if you haven't seen them in years? When your direct reports are engaged and committed to bringing their whole selves to work, there's no limit to what your team—and your company—can accomplish.

▶ QUESTIONS FOR REFLECTION ◀

Below are 18 questions I give to my coaching clients to ask their direct reports so they can better understand what drives them. I recommend you ask them at the start of the working relationship and then in quarterly one-on-ones. But remember, feedback should never be limited to these intensive sit-downs. Feedback should be ongoing and flow both ways between you and your direct reports. Ask them:

1. What is your biggest strength at work?

2. What do you like most about your current role?

3. What do you see your primary responsibilities as?

4. How would you describe these responsibilities?

5. What do you want to accomplish in the next 30/60/90 days?

6. What do you want to accomplish in the next 12 months?

7. What do you perceive my expectations of you to be this year?

8. How will you measure your success?

9. What are your expectations of me as your manager?

10. What gives you the biggest sense of achievement?

11. What is most inspiring about your work?

12. Why is it the most inspiring? (Don't assume what they tell you in question 11 is the answer you will receive here. Inquire a little further.)

13. How do you prefer to be recognized for your achievements?

14. Is there something you would like to learn at work? Any ideas on where or how you can learn this skill? Why is this important to you?

15. How often would you like to meet to discuss how things are going?

16. Would you like to learn from anyone in the organization?

17. How can we best measure your progress here?

18. Is there anything else you would like to add that would help me know you better or help us work together better?

Then you can ask some broader questions during a quarterly follow-up:

▶ **QUESTIONS FOR REFLECTION** ◀

▶ How would you describe the last three months?

▶ What do you want to achieve in the next 30/60/90 days?

▶ How and who will help you reach those goals?

▶ What do you need from me to help you succeed?

Taking the time to have these conversations communicates to employees that you view them as active partners in the organization and in their own development. You don't expect them to carry out marching orders from on high. Instead, you recognize that people do their best work when they are invited to engage on every level, both personal and professional.

Chapter 10

Elephant: Your Workplace Isn't Safe for All Employees

"Diversity" has become a buzzword in recent years. CEOs and hiring managers have launched countless diversity trainings and hiring initiatives. This interest in diversity stems from a positive place: We know that if we look around our workplace and see only one type of person, our company is at a disadvantage. Diverse people bring diverse thinking and diverse solutions to complex problems.

Yet a stated commitment to "diversity" isn't enough to ensure that workplaces are equitable and welcoming to people from all different walks of life. It's not enough to simply say,

"We have X number of this type of person and X number of this type of person, so we're a diverse organization." But this is, unfortunately, often what diversity comes down to: people counting. There's an obsession with numbers, making sure the company has a certain number of a certain type of people.

Rather than focusing on shallow, numbers-based diversity initiatives, people leaders should work to ensure their companies are places where all employees feel (and actually are) safe and included. Diversity without inclusion is harmful. Employees who come from minority backgrounds must feel supported and safe before they can be free to express themselves personally and professionally. In this chapter, we'll examine how people leaders can make their organizations a place where *all* employees can flourish.

What All Leaders Should Ask Themselves

Do all people in your organization feel safe and included? Are employees from diverse backgrounds free to do their work without being marginalized? Is the CEO committed to continually learning about employees with a different life experience from his own? Do you constantly work to broaden your hiring pool?

People leaders who are committed to creating diverse, inclusive work spaces must ask themselves these questions. Yet before you can answer them in any meaningful way, the company's leadership must have an open mind and an eagerness to learn. The CEO and the rest of the C-suite must be humble and willing to be educated on areas in which they have blind spots.

Let's do a thought experiment. Imagine that if you're a CEO or in your company's leadership, you are a white man. Statistically, this is most likely to be the case. In 2018, there were only 24 female CEOs in the Fortune 500 (down from 32 the previous year), and there were only three black CEOs, all of whom were male. The remaining 95 percent of CEOs in the Fortune 500 were white men. Thus, it's a relatively safe assumption that your company leadership is white and male. These numbers have to change if workplaces are going to be a true representation of the world we live in. But for the time being, let's go with the most likely scenario. If you're a white man and your C-suite is largely white and male, what are you doing to educate yourselves about the experiences of those who don't share your position of privilege?

What We Can Learn from Starbucks

When I think of a company that takes seriously its commitment to educating itself on others' experiences, I think of Starbucks. In 2017, Starbucks was recognized as one of the top places to work for LGBTQ individuals, scoring a perfect 100 on the Corporate Equality Index (CEI). For more than 20 years, Starbucks has offered health insurance coverage to employees in lesbian and gay relationships. Starbucks also has workplace gender transition guidelines to support employees who are transgender or who are considering transitioning.

But in 2018, an incident in a Philadelphia Starbucks made news worldwide when a store manager called the police on two black men who were simply waiting to meet a friend. Video footage of the men—clearly posing no threat, complying with police officers—went viral and sparked outrage. Heated calls for customers to boycott Starbucks went all around the internet.

Starbucks CEO Howard Schultz issued an apology for the actions of the store manager (who is no longer with the company). Most leaders would stop here: apologize, hope the story is pushed from the news cycle quickly, and move on. But Schultz showed a deeper commitment to learning about the experience. He also wanted to educate his employees so they would not continue to perpetuate racism and that social media would scrutinize Starbucks morals even further if not rectified through training store-wide.

On May 29, 2018, all 8,000 Starbucks stores in the U.S. were closed for several hours while Schultz and the Starbucks leadership held a companywide training session on racial bias issues. To develop the training, they enlisted black leaders who are experts on race in America: civil rights lawyer and activist Bryan Stevenson, the rapper Common, and president of Ariel Investments and Starbucks board member Mellody Hobson. The training was interactive. It used video, conversation, and role-playing. Schultz said on *CBS This Morning*, "This is not an expense. This is an investment in our people, in our way of life, in our culture and our values."

His actions communicated far more than an apology ever could. Moreover, they showed a true commitment to inclusion and creating a safe space for all.

It's important to note that Starbucks had *already* made the commitment to safety and inclusion for its employees. From this space, Starbucks committed to employee education so that this same level of inclusion could be extended to its customers. As a people leader, how are you educating yourself and your teams about the needs of historically marginalized people groups? Are you actively seeking unicorns from diverse backgrounds—and not just to fill a quota?

Recruit Diverse Unicorns, Then Aim for True Inclusion

Recruiting is a great place to start. "Hiring Across All Spectrums," a 2018 report from Pride at Work Canada, a nonprofit organization that represents LGBTQ union members and their allies, stated the importance of recruiters undergoing training *specifically* about LGBTQ people and their experiences to understand the challenges LGBTQ people encounter in the work force. Training of this nature would help recruiters use correct, inoffensive language, which can go a long way toward establishing trust and building relationships. Respondents surveyed in the Pride at Work report revealed other things companies can do to ensure that a workplace is LGBTQ-friendly. These included:

▶ publicizing all LGBTQ-related policies (such as anti-discrimination policies and gender-transition guidelines);
▶ stating explicitly that a company is LGBTQ-friendly;
▶ having staff undergo LGBTQ-specific training;
▶ and advertising job postings in LGBTQ media.

Recruiters provide potential unicorns with the first taste of your employer brand. If a recruiter uses noninclusive language, the candidate will assume that this reflects the organization's views, and diverse candidates will take their talents elsewhere. (Recall, for example, the sexist tech recruiters from Chapter 4.)

Diverse candidates also won't stay if they're not truly safe within the organization. Even the most immovable, traditionally noninclusive industries are finally waking up to this. This was brought home to me in February 2018 when I attended the DICE (Design, Innovate, Create, Entertain) gaming summit. It was evident that the games industry is taking giant strides toward becoming more equitable for all employees. My heart leapt for joy when Phil Spencer, vice president of gaming at Microsoft, delivered the keynote—which was all about how Microsoft is working to become a more diverse, inclusive, and safe working environment. The five steps he outlined were:

1. Building *empathy and trust* with employees by listening to and honoring their concerns
2. Taking *accountability* as a leader and owning previous mistakes
3. Having a *growth mindset* in which leadership recognizes that failure—public or private—paves the way for growth
4. *Listening* to all voices in the room and *amplifying* those that may not be heard
5. Keeping at the forefront the three *leadership principles* of creating clarity, generating energy for the team, and delivering success

Spencer's keynote was a clear turning point. I'm a veteran of the gaming industry. I have firsthand experience with its rampant sexism; over the years, I've amassed a collection of my own #MeToo stories, and so has every woman I know. In 2017, a study from UK games industry trade body, The Independent Game Developers Association (TIGA), found only 14 percent of the people working in the gaming industry in that country are women. According to the International Game Developers Association (IGDA), more than 75 percent of game developers are white. For women or minorities who have worked in a field dominated by white men, these are more than just statistics. When an organization has extremely high levels of gender and racial disparity, discriminatory language and marginalization of minorities is almost a given.

This is why I was overjoyed to hear Phil Spencer speak so passionately about what Microsoft is doing. What's more, he was using my executive coaching language! I was so excited I went around practically grabbing other conference attendees by the collar and asking them what their organizations were doing to create safe workplaces.

How Organizations Become More Inclusive

Neela Dass, director of game developer relations at Intel, told me her team hosts workshops that help participants identify their unexamined, beneath-the-surface biases and how these biases impact others. Google has a similar training program. Google VP Phil Harrison shared that during its onboarding process, Google trains new employees to better identify their unconscious biases. And I talked to a CEO about how his company lives out its mission to *entertain the world*: Every January the CEO asks his HR Director for an employee overview by race, gender, and gaming ability. These statistics inform future hiring practices and ensures the employees are actually representative of gamers.

I am sometimes struck by how very far we've come. When I began my career in the early 1990s, the workplace was, in a lot of ways, the wild west. There wasn't a structural understanding of why diversity was important, to say nothing of inclusion and the need for safe work spaces. "Political correctness" was largely scoffed at as cumbersome and tedious. Now we know better. The words we use to describe people and things inform how we think and feel about them. By taking care to use language that is free of bias, we are forced to examine our own biases, which are often unconscious. This awareness is the first step toward eliminating our prejudices and developing a truly inclusive worldview.

But we've probably all embarrassed ourselves by using the wrong term for a people group besides our own. How can we get it right when it feels like we can't keep up with the pace of social change?

The bad news is that you almost certainly will say something that makes you feel stupid. The good news is that if you have good-faith relationships with your direct reports and colleagues, they'll believe you when you say, "I'm so sorry. Please, can you teach me the correct way to talk about this?" Generally, people are happy to educate others if a) they have receptive, thankful listeners and b) they don't have to educate people *all the time*. As a people leader, you set the tone for others in your organization. If you make a mistake and are corrected, now you know what to do going forward. The person who took the time to teach you must see you implementing your new knowledge when talking with employees at every level of the company. If you make work a safe space with your attitude and language—and lay out the clear expectation that everyone else will do the same—you show employees from marginalized backgrounds that you have their backs.

CASE STUDY
What We Can Learn from Google

A 2018 lawsuit brought national attention to corporate communications within Google. Engineer James Damore was fired after he wrote a screed against Google's affirmative action and diversity policies. Although he had communicated these thoughts via Google's internal network, the post went viral after it was posted online. Damore then brought a lawsuit against Google in which he cited many of these internal Google conversations. Employees who had been communicating privately among themselves found that their words had a national audience.

A noted part of Google's corporate culture is the tendency for employees to have freewheeling discussions, some related to the job and some not. Damore included screenshots of these discussions in his lawsuit that found their way online. As a result, many of the participants were subjected to online harassment and doxing (when private information, such as a physical address, is revealed without consent). In response, Google CEO Sundar Pichai introduced a new companywide policy specifically prohibiting doxing. In his statement, Pichai noted that although communication between employees takes place on internal channels, Googlers should be wary of how these conversations would appear if made available to the wider public. He added that employees should, "avoid blanket statements about groups or categories of people," and avoid, "trolling, name calling, and ad hominem attacks," stating that the goal of conversations should be to "understand more, not to be right."

What happened at Google is an extreme example, of course. Regardless of your opinion of James Damore, I believe Pichai's response was wise. The goal of the new policy was not to stifle conversations. Rather, it had two aims: to protect employees from harassment and to create the conditions for healthier, more inclusive dialogue.

The Emotional Intelligence Factor

From an emotional intelligence lens, creating an inclusive work environment enhances the *stress-management* component of EQ because it helps employees develop *flexibility*. Flexibility is defined as adapting thoughts, emotions, and behaviors. When we are confronted with the experiences of someone from a different background than our own, we are forced to face any unexamined beliefs we may have held about people from that group. If we are flexible, we can rewire our brains and adapt the way we think, feel, and act. The CEO must model this flexibility. When everyone else sees flexibility at work, it is easier for them to adapt and create a safer work space for employees who are at risk of being marginalized. Employees who feel safe are then free to apply their ingenuity to solving pressing problems.

This rewiring of our brains also improves the *decision-making* component of EQ. Employees who have reckoned with their biases, both conscious and unconscious, are better-equipped to be objective and see things as they really are (the *reality-testing* branch of *decision making*). When we hold prejudices against certain people groups, we can't accurately see the individuals who make up that group. Let's say you have two team members who have difficulty working together. Each mistrusts the other because of conditioning that has taught them to discount the other's value. They are not seeing each other *as they really are*. Instead, they're seeing only their projected biases. Through examining their prejudices, they can move past their preconceived opinions and focus on the work at hand.

If your organization is going to survive and thrive, you need all hands on deck. By maintaining biased hiring practices, you are only harming yourself: People from diverse backgrounds bring different perspectives and experiences that can help you see in a new way.

But it's not enough to merely have a diverse staff. Your workplace must also be inclusive and safe for everyone. Your unicorns will not be at their best in a toxic culture that turns a blind eye to discriminatory language or that is more concerned with maintaining 1950s-style gender norms and dress codes than innovation. If your unicorns are at perpetual risk of marginalization, they must constantly keep their guard up. No high salary, awesome perks package, or generous vacation time will compensate for that.

Your employees deserve better. As a people leader, you set the tone. Know that you're never going to be perfect—that isn't the point. But you can adopt a humble, grateful attitude and commit yourself to always learn about the experiences of others. That attitude is infectious. It can transform your workplace and free up your unicorns to do their best work.

▶ QUESTIONS FOR REFLECTION ◄

Your workplace needs to be inclusive, and your employees need to feel safe. I keep repeating this point because it is so important. Even if you do nothing else I suggest in this book, I advise you to invest the necessary resources (time, money, difficult conversations) to create an inclusive work space. Check in with yourself and your employees to answer the following questions:

▶ Do we have a system that helps employees identify unconscious biases and then work to find solutions?

▶ When's the last time we invested in inclusivity training?

▶ Do employees of all backgrounds feel safe? (You'll have to design a metric to ask them and gauge this.)

▶ When's the last time someone spoke up and said they were uncomfortable with language someone used toward them, with how they were treated, or how other people were treated? What was the response to that person?

▶ What is the retention rate for employees from different backgrounds?

The process of becoming inclusive will involve some difficult conversations. That is OK. Adopt a posture of humble listening and learning. Be grateful for what your employees teach you, even if it feels uncomfortable. On the other side of discomfort is growth. You owe it to your employees to grow into a leader who makes sure their personhood comes first at work.

Chapter 11

Elephant: You're Cagey About Negotiation

If you're like a lot of people, the title of this chapter sent some shivers up your spine. *Negotiation.* People whisper the word as if they're afraid to speak it aloud. Candidates and hiring managers alike shy away from it.

But negotiation is not a dirty word—it's a normal, healthy part of any hiring process. As such, the negotiation process must take place out in the open between the hiring manager and the candidate. It's not something to be pawned off on a recruiter or ignored altogether. Open and frank negotiation during the hiring process—and as needed once the new hire is in place—builds trust between the employee and the organization.

But there's a right way and a wrong way to approach negotiation. In the wrong way, the hiring manager will post a job with absolutely no clues as to the salary range. Let's say the company is hiring a CEO, and the description only says something about the salary being "executive level."

The problem is that the meaning of "executive level" can vary wildly across industries. Perhaps one executive sees the posting and thinks the position looks promising. She is currently making $600K and believes this job will have similar compensation. When she finally talks salary— probably in the third or fourth interview—she is shocked to learn that the top compensation is $250K. The discussion is terminated; both parties have wasted each other's time.

The fact is that candidates are becoming savvier. Job postings don't rank as high in Google if they don't include a salary range. Candidates who want to know a range for their industry or a specific company just need to visit Glassdoor. People leaders and hiring managers should expect that any self-respecting candidate has done his homework and knows the approximate salary range for the job.

Yet we're still squeamish about the concept of negotiation. Often we view it as a zero-sum game. The hiring manager believes she has to keep the salary card close to the vest to be revealed only at the last moment. The candidate's needs are not front and center. Rather, the hiring manager is thinking of everything she hopes to "get" out of the new hire for the desired price and hoping like heck the new hire will go along with it. Four outcomes are possible in this scenario:

1. The candidate agrees happily and is only slightly annoyed he didn't know the number earlier in the process.
2. The candidate agrees begrudgingly. It's lower than he hoped.
3. The candidate wishes to negotiate. From there, both parties play a game of "cat and mouse," where only one side can come out a winner.
4. The candidate walks away, sorry to have wasted so much of his time.

The first three scenarios result in the candidate being hired, but none build good faith. Imagine the candidate's thinking throughout this process. By not discussing salary openly from the beginning, the hiring manager has turned it into an elephant. Whether or not she feels it, the new hire she so desperately wants to win over does. He's been thinking, *When are we going to talk money?* since the first interview, but he hasn't brought it up out of politeness. By *not* being clear about the salary range, the hiring manager has taken advantage of the candidate's good manners.

In this chapter, you'll learn how to stop making negotiations so awkward. We'll also see how it can be a win-win for you and your new hire. It ought to be. In fact, I'll go so far to say that anything less than a "win-win" situation is actually a loss—and probably not a road you want to go down.

How Negotiation Can Be a Win-Win

Instead of viewing negotiation as a zero-sum game, try thinking of it as a collaborative process. Both parties should assume good intent. The candidate understands the job that's being asked of him and how he could use his talents to best serve the company, while the hiring manager understands the candidate's needs. Both know the standard market rates for the position because everyone has done their homework. Instead of seeing who comes out "on top," they collaborate and work together to craft a deal. Both are clear about their needs and wants throughout the process. If hiring manager and candidate can arrive at a salary that suits both their needs, fantastic. If not, the candidate departs with no hard feelings.

A 2019 survey conducted by staffing firm Robert Half found that only 68 percent of men and 45 percent of women negotiated for higher salaries when receiving a job offer. What does this tell us? First, many job seekers are not taking advantage of the candidates' market. Second, women still negotiate less than men. Many studies have shown that women are more likely to advocate for others than to speak out on behalf of themselves. Third, it's worth it for candidates to push past their discomfort and negotiate for their full worth. Bonuses and raises are calculated from base salary, so a candidate who does not negotiate for a higher base salary is leaving money on the table more than once.

On the other side of the table, you should expect a unicorn to negotiate. Likewise, as a people leader, you need to talk dollars and cents as early in the process as possible. It's the only way to have any kind of substantive discussion with a unicorn.

Don't make the mistake of the CEO above, who was unpleasantly surprised to learn that her "dream job" came with a 350-percent pay cut. Is the job commission-based with no base salary? You absolutely need to ask as soon as possible. Recall my experience with my employee Rebecca in Chapter 8. I could have saved both of us a lot of unpleasantness if we'd had more frank conversations about pay structure from the very beginning.

This is something I feel so passionately about that I'd shout it from the rooftops if I could: *Don't have a third party conduct a salary negotiation.* In my experience, a recruiter discussing salary immediately puts the candidate on edge. A better practice is to bring the hiring manager into the discussion at this point or even the CEO if the company is small.

For example, recently I was placing a candidate, Morgan, and we finally got around to talking money. I could tell she was slightly uneasy about bringing it up. "What kind of package do you think they'll offer me?" Morgan asked.

"How about I get the CEO in on this conversation?" I suggested. I could immediately sense her relief over the phone.

If you're a CEO or hiring manager and you're not comfortable having the money talk in the candidate stage, how will you discuss pay raises and bonuses when it's time for the performance review? Having open, frank discussions from the very beginning builds trust. As a recruiter, *I* wasn't going to be the one paying Morgan. Even if you have the best damn recruiter in the world placing a candidate, you *still* don't want her talking salary. A recruiter's role is primarily transactional. At the end of the day, she gets her placement check for finding the talent—and then she's gone. You don't want someone with such a short-term stake in the hiring process conducting salary discussions with your candidate, who you hope will be there for the long run.

Don't Leave Your Would-Be Unicorns Hanging

Remember—you're aiming for a happy marriage between candidate and organization, so you want all your cards on the table from the very beginning. The fact is that great candidates have some *very* attractive options out there. Giants like Google, Netflix, and Facebook woo top talent with incredible stock options, flex time, onsite day care, etc. How are you going to compete with that? Do your would-be unicorns sense that company leadership is willing to go the extra mile for them?

If you're crazy about a candidate, you have to show that, and it will not get through if you have a third party conducting salary negotiations. For critical hires, you have to get the key players involved. This is where not being a Facebook or a Google can actually be beneficial. Smaller companies wooing top talent can offer white-glove treatment—personalized attention and care from the very top. How can you make the candidate feel special? A $50K signing bonus? Freedom to work out of one of the overseas offices at will? Flex time? Working from home two days a week? If a candidate knows you've taken her specific situation into account and are tailoring your offer based on her needs and wants, she will feel special. And as a result, she is more likely to stick around for the long haul.

Recognize that if a unicorn is truly a star, she is likely to get competing offers. So what happens if your newly hired unicorn gets a seemingly unbeatable offer with another company within six months of joining your team? If she tells you about it because she is genuinely unsure which path to choose, what do you do?

Money Isn't Everything

There are lots of reasons people take jobs. Money is important, but it's not everything. What is attractive about the other offer? What are your unicorn's wants and needs for this stage of life? If you've shown her that you care about her well-being and want to support her—both in and outside the office—she may open up and share more details. Even if you can't match the proposed salary, knowing your new hire's true needs may enable you to counteroffer with a package more suitable to her current situation. I've seen plenty of people turn down higher salaries and awesome perks to stay with employers they feel truly have their backs. A giant may be able to offer a "bells and whistles" package that really wows. But relationships are more important. Not every company can create a space in which your unicorn feels truly known and appreciated—but yours *can*.

At the end of the day, it's about respect. A unicorn who feels respected and valued from the beginning will be motivated to do her best work. Respect your key hires enough to have important money conversations with them from the get-go. Recognize that your unicorn is not dumb. (Or why would you want to hire her so badly?) She will sense if you're pawning her off on someone else. When the two of you come to the negotiating table to see what you can do for each other, everybody wins. You really can have it all.

The Emotional Intelligence Factor

There is an emotional intelligence benefit when hiring managers leave the door open for candidates to discuss salary openly. Salary talks engage a candidate's *stress-management* capabilities. *Optimism* falls under this category: A candidate who exerts some control over her salary is likely to feel more positive about the final number and her employer as a whole. Likewise, a candidate who negotiates her salary is engaging the *self-expression* component of EQ, particularly *assertiveness*. A candidate who will assert herself is an asset to an organization. Such an employee will speak up when needed, challenge outdated thinking, and articulate new paths forward.

If a candidate doesn't want to talk salary until later in the process, it's not an immediate issue. Depending on his background and motivations, he may not view it as appropriate. Or perhaps he is coming from the public sector, where exact salaries are searchable online and rarely up for negotiation.

Similarly, as a people leader, you shouldn't fall into the trap of thinking that all your direct reports should be exactly like you. Say you're incredibly ambitious and stay awake at night dreaming of ways to double, triple, or quadruple your salary. You should recognize that many candidates will not have this same point of view. That doesn't mean they won't work hard and be high performers—it just means they're not as financially aspirational, and there's absolutely nothing wrong with that. Don't count out a potential unicorn just because she doesn't share your financial goals.

> ▸ **QUESTIONS FOR REFLECTION** ◂

The only way to truly evaluate how well you handle negotiation is by getting feedback from your employees. Until you know what it's like on *their* end of the hiring dance, you won't have a good read on how well the process is working. To get clear on this, do the following:

- ▸ Identify hires who joined your organization one month, one year, and two years ago.
- ▸ Ask them: What doubts did you experience during the offer stage?
- ▸ What would have made you accept faster?

If the negotiation process was awkward for your unicorns, ask them to tell you why. It may even be worth contacting a former candidate who signed with a competitor instead of you. Get a clear picture of the situation by looking at it from all angles. Your commitment to improving the negotiation process will pay off in the next round of hiring.

Chapter 12

Elephant: You and Your Key Hires Don't Receive Coaching

B ack in my early 20s, before I officially began my career at Virgin, I found myself between jobs. As a stopgap, I got hired on at The Body Shop, of all places. Anyone who's worked in retail knows the annoyances that come with the job: rude customers, repetitive work, long hours on your feet. I was less than enthusiastic about it. But then my manager asked me to take on a new responsibility: masseuse. Baby masseuse, specifically.

The Body Shop was hosting workshops for new mothers to teach them how to give massages to soothe and connect with their babies. My manager thought I would be a great choice to lead them though this was years before I became a mother myself. I said yes without the slightest clue what I was signing on for—at least it was a break from the tedium of retail. Instead of being on the floor, I got to huddle in a back room and pore over the ins and outs of the massage technique until it was time to teach in front of real live mothers and their real live babies. These ladies would actually hand *me* their babies to demonstrate on. I was exhilarated. I was also terrified!

But pretty soon, I felt like an absolute *rock star*. The massages were actually working. The babies were happy! Seeing the relief and gratitude on these desperate mothers' faces made me feel like a million bucks. Here I was, actually improving women's lives with a tool, rather than just folding merchandise and ringing up customers. Because of *my* class, these women were learning how to be better connected to their babies and to inhabit their new roles as mothers more comfortably. I got a high you can't buy.

However unexpected, my experience at The Body Shop provided me with my first foray into coaching, and I discovered that I absolutely loved it. I loved studying the material until I knew it inside and out (God forbid I screw up and hurt a baby!) and then translating that knowledge into practical assistance to help these mothers in their "jobs."

I believe that receiving coaching is transformational. It's the quickest way to grow, personally and professionally. In this chapter, we'll examine how you and your teams can level up by investing in coaching.

Everyone Needs a Coach

This is something I believe in the marrow of my bones: *Everyone* needs a coach.

New moms need a coach. Recruiters need a coach. CEOs need a coach. Hiring managers need a coach. *Coaches* need a coach. In the words of Google CEO Eric Schmidt, "The one thing people are never good at is seeing themselves as others see them. A coach really, really helps." For that reason alone, it's vital that CEOs receive coaching as they lead their organizations and that they bring the rest of leadership along with them.

The company's leadership must be on the same page as they seek to "know what they don't know." With the help of an objective third party, they can identify and overcome any blind spots.

Only someone who's removed from the ins and outs of your company can help you evolve to the next level. A coach who isn't directly involved in your workplace politics can see situations clearly and provide useful feedback. Recall my experience with Anthony and Henry in Chapter 9. Henry was unable to see how the massive earthquakes at the company had deeply unsettled Anthony in his first 100 days. He was too focused on the bottom line to have enough mental space to consider the human aspect. Had I not been there as an objective third party, confusion and frustration would have continued to reign.

CASE STUDY
Tom and the Looming Culture Clash

I saw the potential for internal disruption with one of the first candidates I ever placed at the beginning of my headhunting career, back when I still needed to prove to myself that I could do the job. We'll call the candidate Tom. I was so pleased when I placed him with a promising organization. His skill set matched the position well; the company was grateful to have him, and the salary was fantastic. Tom went to work with the new organization, and everyone went merrily on their way.

Yet I was deeply unsatisfied. The more I thought about Tom's placement, the less well it sat with me. Tom was unknowingly walking into a potentially tumultuous situation—the leadership of the company was Italian, and I knew their working style was quite different than what Tom, an American, was used to. Plus, the job was in the UK—a *triple* culture shock. *I knew this*. But I didn't think Tom had been adequately briefed on the work environment for which he was totally uprooting his life. I began to feel more and more uneasy—even guilty. Did Tom have any idea what he had signed up for? Could I have done more to prepare him?

I knew Tom needed more than the services I could offer at the time, and it gnawed at me. What was lacking was coaching, yet I wasn't equipped to offer it to him at the time (this was before I obtained my Executive Coaching Certificate, Professional Certified Coach (PCC) accreditation, and EQ-i 2.0 practitioner qualifications). Later, when I launched FORWARD, I saw the need to have an integrated coaching branch so we could set our clients on track for the most success possible.

You're likely familiar with the grim statistics regarding CEO retention: There's about a 50-percent chance that a CEO will leave within the first 18 months. This rapid rate of turnover causes stock values to plummet, shareholders to get antsy, and employees to become frustrated. How is your company ever going to move forward if you can't retain people, especially in leadership?

Hiring a member of the executive team *without* a coach would be akin to a football team signing a quarterback and then leaving him to figure things out on his own. That would be madness. It's imperative that executives have someone to guide them through the transition—and someone not connected to the bottom line.

Beware Unconscious Incompetency

When Dr. Ulrik Juul Christensen was a guest on my podcast, he talked about "unconscious incompetencies." As the term suggests, unconscious incompetencies are the things we don't know we don't know. Addressing and removing unconscious incompetence is the cause to which he has dedicated his life. According to data collated by Christensen's educational software company Area9 Lyceum, whose mission it is to "deliver the world's best educational and training outcomes validated by a long-term scientific approach," people are unconsciously incompetent in 20 to 40 percent of their field of expertise. That doesn't mean they're totally competent on the other 60 to 80 percent. On quite a bit of other information, these "experts" may be *knowingly* incompetent. But for up to 40 percent of the *key* knowledge required to execute their jobs properly, people don't even know that they don't have the necessary information.

Christensen has also noted a disturbing trend: The higher up the ladder someone climbs, the more unconscious incompetencies exist. These more senior people are often the ones who train and teach the more junior staff. This means they are passing on incorrect information, which the junior staff then pass on in their circles, and on and on. Imagine you were having a strange physical symptom and went to a hospital. The attending physician gave you a diagnosis that, ultimately, proved to be incorrect. Yet he passed on this faulty information to hundreds of young medical students who may see—and misdiagnose—the illness in their own practices one day. Clearly, we have a problem.

Christensen is dedicated to first addressing unconscious incompetence and then removing it. He works to develop online corporate training programs that encourage people to say when they don't know something. These modules also require trainees to rate their level of confidence when answering questions. For instance, participants can say whether they're absolutely sure of their answer, whether they *think* they have the right answer, or if they're taking a wild stab at it. It's an approach that addresses incompetence with curiosity rather than judgment. People are not penalized for not knowing something; rather, they're invited to go deeper where they are unsure.

If we had this type of environment in the corporate world—if we could lose our rigid belief system that says we're never allowed to make a mistake—we would save so much time. We could admit mistakes, address them, and find collaborative solutions. Owning our humanity allows us to take our armor off and get to the heart of the matter.

Coaching: A Safe Space for Professional Growth

Part of the solution to changing our way of thinking is feedback, as we discussed in Chapter 8. Executives must receive feedback publicly. A powerful leader can admit to her team that she doesn't know something and is open to suggestion and correction. If your team members see you admitting that you don't know everything, they'll be more likely to acknowledge their own areas of ignorance and ask for help when they need it.

Yet even in the ideal workplace, where the boss gives and receives feedback, colleagues lean on one another, and no one has unconscious incompetencies, a coach is still invaluable. A coach can see the forest, not the trees. An executive who can discuss every aspect of his job freely and openly with a coach will gain a clearer picture of the organization, his role within it, and what strategies will help him achieve the success he desires.

As leaders, we need to get over our need to be right. The smartest, most innovative people I know are the ones who can utter three simple words: "I don't know." In a negotiation or meeting, I trust the person who tells me she doesn't know something but will find the answer. When the person doesn't know the answer and is bluffing, or is too arrogant to admit he doesn't know, my radar gets twitchy and my trust is lost. As a leader, are you more concerned with *being* right or *getting it* right?

These two options may sound similar, but there's a world of difference between them. A boss concerned with *being* right wants to be The Source: the almighty dispenser of decisions and plans, the savior, the chosen one. A boss concerned with *getting it* right is open to ideas and solutions, wherever they come from. The second type of leader knows that good ideas can come from anyone, anywhere, at any time. His approach is collaborative and loose. If he gets it wrong, he can admit he screwed up and course-correct as he goes. The stakes are lower for him, so there's room for experimentation, risk-taking, and ultimately reward.

This is where coaching comes in. In the coach-mentee relationship, there is also space for experimentation (even play!). The mentee is answering to a peer professional—not a boss. If you as a mentee "screw up," who cares? Mistakes are inevitable. They're also how you grow. In the coaching relationship, that dynamic is understood. There's no need for a mentee to stick her tail between her legs and worry about how a mistake will affect the bottom line. Mistakes are made, acknowledged, and learned from. Such an atmosphere accelerates growth.

In my ideal world, every people leader of every organization would deep dive with a coach weekly, at least for the first 100 days and then as needed throughout his or her tenure. (When I say people leader here, I mean a C-suite member or other key hire in a significant leadership position.) Such support would increase the leader's effectiveness in powerful ways. He wouldn't run for the exit sign as soon as his head began to slip underwater (for some leaders, that's on day one), and he would feel less isolated. Isolation is one of the biggest problems facing the modern workplace, from entry-level employees all the way on up to the CEO. The people in the C-suite are no different from anyone else, and it's lonely at the top. A leader able to check in regularly with a coach gains a unique support system. Unlike employees, the coach's financial future is not riding on whether the executive succeeds or fails. The coach is a leadership confidante offering a close connection, guidance, a safe space to find solutions openly—whatever the executive needs as he attempts to navigate the tricky business of taking over the operations of a company.

Second, a people leader reporting to a coach is committing to a growth mindset. He goes in acknowledging that he cannot do or know everything by himself. He has limitations, blind spots, areas in which he can improve. He is investing in his personal development because he realizes it's the smartest thing to do for the company. A leader with this attitude realizes that his employees can grow as well. He can lead the organization in adopting a mindset in which there is freedom to take risks and think outside the box. In a growth mindset, there is an understanding that people, roles, goals, etc. are always evolving. No person is ever "fixed"; there is always room for improvement.

Third, a people leader with a coach retains an openness he does not have if his entire world is constrained to the organization. It's easy to get tunnel vision. A new leader, who may have been hired to turn the ship around, is very likely stepping into chaos. Everything then becomes about producing value for shareholders. He can easily become consumed with what's needed that day/month/quarter. In this mode, the leader essentially becomes a firefighter, staying busy just putting out fires throughout the day. There is no space for him to pause, step back, and think creatively about solutions. That's where a coach can help.

The Emotional Intelligence Factor

A coach is a partner—with a coach, the leader is not alone. A coach provides perspective, clarity, and out-of-the-box thinking. A coach enables a people leader to break out of the pattern of constantly feeling stressed. The coaching relationship is collaborative, innovative, fresh; an executive can then transmit this energy and reinvigorate the entire company.

A people leader who recognizes that she needs a coach boasts strong *self-perception*. *Self-regard*, one of the pillars of the *self-perception* component of EQ, is defined as respecting oneself while respecting oneself; having confidence. The better a leader is in touch with her strengths and weaknesses, the more able she is to help the larger organization. Another pillar of *self-perception* is *self-actualization*, or the pursuit of meaning or self-improvement. Few things are more dangerous to organizations (or, frankly, to society as a whole) than people who are unwilling to evolve.

As we step fully into the fourth industrial revolution, coaches are more important than ever. We know that adaptable companies are the ones with a shot at survival. Organizations must embrace the AI age and recognize that individual roles will change as AI becomes more prominent in the workplace. This ability to adapt has to come from the top. The CEO must model adaptability and flexibility. Moreover, a people leader who works with a coach realizes that together, we are more than we are alone. Agile teams are better able to respond to changing work force currents. A leader linked to a coach has one more team member to help them weather whatever storms are on the horizon.

A know-it-all attitude can sink a company and send would-be unicorns scurrying for the exits. Yet when a people leader cares enough about the organization to delve into his own unconscious incompetencies and receive guidance, he positions himself to blow past limits and experience exponential growth. When this growth happens on the organizational level, the potential is boundless.

▶ QUESTIONS FOR REFLECTION ◀

Is embracing a learning mindset a priority at your organization? Answer the questions below honestly to gauge how you're doing in developing yourself and your employees.

▶ When was the last time you invested in coaching for yourself?

▶ Do your key hires receive coaching? If yes, for how long?

▶ If you integrate coaching, how successful has it been? How do your key hires report on their experiences? How has their work improved (or not)?

▶ Do you have regular, company-wide professional development for employees at ALL levels?

▶ How effective have these sessions been? (What do your employees report? Do you have a metric by which you can gauge their honest feedback? Do these sessions address gaps you see in the companywide skill set—and is there improvement afterward?)

▶ QUESTIONS FOR REFLECTION ◀

I would never recommend implementing coaching or professional development for its own sake. That's the equivalent of filling out endless worksheets for "busy work" in school. Rather, sit down and determine what key objectives you would like to achieve *before* working with a coach. Do the same with your key hires. Begin with the end in mind: Figure out your desired result, and then seek out a coach you trust who can help get you there.

Chapter 13

Elephant: You're Addicted to Busy

When I'm in "addicted to busyness" mode, my days look something like this:

▶ Wake up and check emails for ten minutes before I'm even out of bed.

▶ Rush to get the kids ready for school while I scarf down a banana or a granola bar and then race out the door.

▶ Arrive at work; have about 10 minutes to gather myself before it's time for a meeting.

▶ Throughout the day: several one- to two-hour-long meetings with me checking my email in between.

- ▶ Touch base to see what's on the docket with clients to ensure I'm ready for our sessions.
- ▶ Rush home, interact with family amid more email, hop in bed, and perform one last phone scan.
- ▶ Sleep, wake up, and start the cycle over again.

Sound familiar?

It's a conundrum: As we reach the executive level, more and more demands are placed on our time. Days are filled with meetings: performance reviews, client pitches, and department head strategy sessions. If you're at the top, it's likely that every minute of your day is accounted for before you even set foot in the office.

But the higher you rise, the more important it is to have space for strategic thinking. Staying constantly in "hamster wheel" mode means you can meet the demands of the day but not much else. How can you be the visionary your organization needs if you never have time for a vision? If your schedule leaves no room for the rest and play that are the birthplace of creativity, how will you explore innovative ways to lead the organization forward?

In this chapter, I'm going to help you unpack and unload the burden of "busy" and the effect it can have on you and your company. After all, if everyone on your team is as #crazybusy as you are, imagine what that does for overall morale and productivity. It can be like a whole herd of elephants, frightening away even the most magical unicorns.

Break Your Busyness Addiction and Reclaim Your Creativity

Our addiction to constant busyness is partly a failure of imagination. We simply can't conceive that another way is possible. I loved Rasmus Hougaard and Jacqueline Carter's 2018 book *The Mind of the Leader*, which thoroughly explores the concept of "action addiction." When speaking on this same topic, entrepreneur and strategy consultant Dorie Clark has observed that we measure "busyness" as a sign of social status, substituting working long hours for real loyalty and productivity.

Bingo. We tell ourselves that the only way to get ahead is to always be working. We tell ourselves this even if we *know* our work suffers after a certain threshold (also known as the point of diminishing returns). Research backs this up; according to a 2014 study by John Pencavel, an economics professor at Stanford University, productivity decreases for people who work more than 50 hours a week. Productivity for a 70-hour work week was basically the same as that for a 56-hour week; workers might as well have gone home for those extra 14 hours! Yet for most professionals, the idea of the 40-hour workweek is long past; 50 hours is the base line. Maybe you're reading this while working 60, 70, or 80 hours per week. Working *only* 50 hours a week may sound like a pipe dream!

Lately, "mindfulness" has become a buzzword. Ten years ago, mindfulness seemed like something reserved for Buddhist monks rather than a practice for everyday people to draw on. These days, *everyone* is talking mindfulness. Only we're not exactly sure what it means. We just know we're supposed to move more *mindfully* through our days. I'm glad the term has come into more common usage. But if you're like me, the concept can stress you out! I've got a to-do list a mile long, and I'm supposed to add "be mindful" to it? Maybe I'll swap out my afternoon coffee for tea and try to savor it for 30 seconds. Then I'll dive back into my email.

If this sounds familiar to you, know you're not alone. Breaking the cycle of busy addiction is *hard*. Breaking any addiction is hard. But being addicted to something doesn't feel good. Being tethered to the tasks on your to-do list means you're not in control of your day. Even if you're the CEO of a large organization, you're still essentially employed by your email.

How do you want to *feel* as you move through your day? Do you enjoy that lightheaded buzzy feeling you get from chronic stress, never quite feeling like you've got both feet on the ground? Do you like the hollow pit in your stomach from the time you wake up until it's lights out? I can think of many adjectives to describe addiction, but enjoyable is not one of them. Most of us are used to our calendars dictating our mood and our stress dictating our emotions. But we can actually have it the other way around.

To enhance the *stress-management* component of emotional intelligence, people leaders must take some time away from the tasks at hand. More is not always more—spending more time at your desk slogging through task after task does not create a fertile environment for innovative thinking. People leaders who have systems in place to increase their *stress tolerance*, a pillar of *stress management* that helps them cope with stressful situations, are better able to lead their teams. Taking care of our mental states and handling our emotions as they arise prevents our stress from leaking downward to our direct reports and creating more problems.

Strategies for Breaking Your Busyness Addiction

I agree with Rasmus Hougaard and Jacqueline Carter's recommendation that leaders block out an hour a day for focused work and thinking. This time is sacred: During this hour, you are unavailable to attend meetings or put out fires. The shape this hour takes is up to you. If a good, long run is the best way to clear your head, put on your running shoes and take off around the city. Or perhaps you find clarity through journaling or meditation. Maybe you simply hang the "do not disturb" sign on your office door for an hour so you can do the focused, deep work necessary for insight and innovation. It doesn't matter *what* you do to rein in the racing horses in your mind. What's important is that you *do* it. Regularly and consistently.

Another method I find invaluable for working without distractions is a timer (you can use the alarm function on your smartphone). I set a timer for 40 minutes each morning. During that time, I'm not allowed to check my emails or text messages, read an interesting article on LinkedIn— nothing. I can only focus on the task at hand. Forty minutes, to me, is a manageable chunk of time during which I can tune out all the noise of the world. Once the timer dings, it's all still there where I left it.

There are loads of other tricks you can try to bring a measure of calm back into your day. Set a shorter timer for five minutes (or even one!). While the timer's going, turn away from all your screens. Focus on your breath. Any time your mind wanders, bring it back to the *in-out, in-out* of your breathing. It's the simplest form of meditation, but it's incredibly helpful in calming your heart rate and focusing your mind. Even such a short reset can have enormous benefits for your concentration and energy levels.

Float Sessions: My Favorite Mind Cleanser

In 2015, I discovered my favorite way to clear my mind: float sessions. It was more than just work stress that brought me to this unique form of meditation/therapy: At the time, a very close friend was dying of cancer. I wanted to be there for my friend Simon at every step of his journey and for whatever he needed in those last few months of his life. Well-meaning friends and acquaintances rallied around Simon, telling him to "hang in there" and "keep fighting." But dying was incredibly stressful for him. Apart from the disease that was slowly killing him, he was faced with arranging his estate, making an exit plan for work, taking the bucket list trips he'd always dreamed of, etc. There was so much to think about, and I was there with him as he wrestled with much of it.

Life doesn't stop for terminal illness. I was supporting my friend on top of all the other normal things in my schedule: parenting my children, running my business, and being a wife to my husband. When I finally paused to catch my breath, I realized I was deteriorating. If you've ever supported someone with a serious illness or been a caregiver for someone at a vulnerable stage of life—say, a young child or an aging parent—you know how badly the supporter needs support. I needed help. Desperate, I knew I needed to feel urgently calm so I Googled an article on floating that gave me hope. I phoned my local float center, overshared with the poor receptionist about what I was going through, and explained how I needed a session pronto.

The next morning, I was floating weightless in a giant tank filled with saline water at the float center. Deprived of all sensory stimuli, I simply lay there buoyed by saline water allowing my mind—at last—to comforting silence. For a full hour I floated, the anxieties of the previous months melting away one by one. When my time was up, I was hooked. I found the receptionist to whom I'd previously told my life story and bought nine more sessions.

By the time I'd had four more sessions, I felt as if I'd undergone a full year of therapy. Lying weightless in the water flooded my brain with serotonin and dopamine. It took me back to my childhood, when my family were expats in Singapore. I'd spend long, aimless hours by myself, floating at the local pools. Now, the float center was the one place I could shed the stresses of my daily life and truly be still.

What activity does that for you? It's worth it to find the answer to that question and then block off time in your calendar for the activity. Recognize that this brain recharging time will not magically appear in your week. You must purposefully make room in your calendar for it. Also realize that these mental breaks are not selfish—they're necessary. You can't be the leader your teams need you to be if you're not in control of yourself. A leader who is constantly harried and overwhelmed will not inspire confidence in others. Most important, you'll have no confidence in *yourself* if this is your M.O. You've got big goals and benchmarks to meet. You need to bring your A game. Getting caught up in a cycle of action addiction leaves you uncentered and disconnected from your true purpose and power. We should all be aiming for more.

The Emotional Intelligence Factor

You must be aware of a problem before you can solve it. If you recognize that you're caught in an addiction to being busy, acknowledging the situation is your first step toward breaking the cycle. From an emotional intelligence perspective, freedom from your busyness addiction brings tremendous benefits. Let's look at the *stress-management* component of EQ-i 2.0 for some guidance on how to break the busyness cycle. *Flexibility* is one of its three pillars. Leaders who have mental recharge breaks built into their schedules are in a better space to respond to the changing needs around them. Response is key. They are responding to their day, rather than merely reacting to whatever stresses come their way. Leaders with enhanced flexibility stop treating their to-do lists like a holy book. They are open and adaptable; they can discard their preconceived notions of "the right way" to accomplish something and change course if a better way becomes apparent. They also have a lot more fun.

People leaders who are able to manage their stress are also better at *decision making*, another of the five components of EQ-i 2.0. They are better at *problem solving*, one of the three pillars of *decision making*, because they are aware of their emotions and recognize how those emotions are influencing them, positively or negatively. For leaders who *don't* understand the emotions underlying their thought processes, a vague cloud of unease enshrouds them. Here's a tip: Emotions are *always* engaged in decision making. Some people like to claim that they are entirely rational, that they don't need to worry about emotions since all their decisions proceed from logical thought. But this is never true. When you clearly understand your emotions, you can measure their impact on your day-to-day actions.

Another pillar of *decision making* is *reality testing,* the ability to be objective and see things as they really are. People leaders who make time for mental recharges come back to the pressing tasks of the day with a clearer sense of what's what. The further we move from our center, the harder it is to discern what's true and what's false. When I'm uncentered, everything begins to look grim, and problems appear worse than they are. Consequently, my reactions are worse—I'm reacting, not responding. A short break—for meditation, a hike, or a float session—restores my sense of clarity. Problems that seemed insurmountable suddenly have an obvious solution.

The fourth industrial revolution will leave no room for companies that don't make time for strategy. That means you as a people leader have to schedule time for mental clarity that begets strategic thinking—*now.* Harried and stressed people leaders constantly on the hamster wheel are not going to attract top talent. If that is your current condition, recognize that your stress is likely leaking all over your company and driving away potential unicorns.

You *can* break the cycle of busyness addiction. You *can* master your emotions, your to-do list, and your time, even if the tasks seem endless. Once you do, and once you implement steps to break free of action addiction to be the centered, strategic leader your teams need you to be, you (and your company) will be poised to not only survive but thrive.

▸ QUESTIONS FOR REFLECTION ◂

One of the biggest elephants in your boardroom is the addiction to being busy. It affects you personally and professionally, which filters down to your teams. And if you are experiencing to-do list overload, you're probably not the only one. Take some time to take stock of your busyness levels so you can adjust sails and curb your addiction to constant action. Below are some questions to ask yourself. Have your teams do this self-reflection exercise as well so you can help promote a more balanced approach to work.

▸ Do you schedule *at least* 15 minutes of personal time into your daily routine?

▶ QUESTIONS FOR REFLECTION ◀

▶ Are you achieving your desired professional results in 50 hours a week or less? Would you like your working hours to fall within this parameter?

▶ What are some steps you could take to cut down on your hours?

▶ How do you influence people on a good day?

▶ How do you influence people on a bad day?

▶ Are you aware of your stress triggers? Do you regularly work on managing your responses to them?

▶ Are you able to stop work and focus on personal goals?

Chapter 14

Elephant: You Need to Re-Skill Your Teams—But How?

The Moore's Law age is dead; long live the AI age. With decades of AI scaling ahead, we will be evolving faster than ever before. That means it's more important than ever for people leaders to continually invest in their employees to keep a competitive edge in the marketplace. Providing skills-based training isn't "a nicety; it's almost a business imperative," says Bill Pelster, a principal at Deloitte Consulting LLP, in a 2017 conversation with *Talent Economy* magazine. Failing to re-skill your teams means your organization loses its ability to evolve as fast as your competitors. You don't want your employer brand and employees to be dinosaurs.

Yet I see the same problems again and again. Company leadership become overwhelmed by the smorgasbord of new technologies intended to aid their operations, so they don't adopt any of them. Or, on the flip side, the C-suite goes gaga for every shiny new toy that comes on the marketplace, spends loads of money, and fails to properly implement the technology it has just invested in so heavily. When another promising new technology comes along, it's Shiny Object Syndrome all over again.

There are two key components to successfully re-skilling your work force, which I'll outline in the first part of this chapter. Then I'll highlight some technologies that *I'm* truly excited about. The key is to keep your organization's needs in mind when determining which tech to adopt.

Before You Decide to Re-Skill Your Team

The first component of successfully re-skilling your work force is to carefully consider where your organization needs to go. From there, you can determine if you need to implement a new technology or process and develop a plan to re-skill whichever teams most need to adapt. Leaders who take this important first step don't fall into the trap of Shiny Object Syndrome. They deploy strategic thinking and something called *appreciative inquiry* to consider where their organization needs to go and how to get it there.

Let's take a look at the appreciative inquiry model. Appreciative inquiry is a concept developed in the 1980s by David L. Cooperrider and Suresh Srivastva, both professors at Case Western Reserve University. It is a tool people leaders use for organizational improvement; they do this not by focusing on "problems" that need to be solved, but rather by appreciating the resources already available within a group of people and examining how those resources may be engaged for positive change. Appreciative inquiry consists of five components (read more at appreciativeinquiry.champlain.edu):

1. *Define*—What is the topic of inquiry? What needs to be achieved?
2. *Discover*—Appreciating the best of "what is." This is an opportunity for you to remember and celebrate your company's successes and strengths.

3. *Dream*—Imagining "what could be." After considering what the organization is doing well, this is a chance to dream of how your company could further improve.

4. *Design*—Determining "what should be." Combine the best of what is and the best of what could be to determine "what should be."

5. *Deliver/Destiny*—Creating "what will be." This identifies how the design will be delivered, adopted, and implemented across groups.

This framework is tremendously helpful for people leaders seeking to determine which technologies and human systems would best evolve their organizations. I like it because it takes such a positive approach to change. Rather than thinking, "Oh no! We've got to change everything or we're going to be left behind by our competitors," appreciative inquiry invites leaders to first consider what their companies are doing right. The focus is on moving from *good* to *better*. There's a saying I'm fond of: "Terrified people make terrible decisions." If you're stressed out and scared, you're likely to make bad decisions when it comes to implementing new technology and re-skilling your work force (or you'll make the equally bad mistake of not getting your employees' buy-in when it comes time to make the change). I find that appreciative inquiry helps dispel some of the fear that is often present whenever big changes are on the horizon.

Leaders considering implementing organizational change with the appreciative inquiry model might ask questions along these lines:

▶ What is working well?
▶ Where do we need to go?
▶ Which service are we currently providing that is likely to be automated soon?
▶ How can we re-skill the workers performing that job function into another area that will provide added value to the company?

This approach values everyone in your organization and celebrates the successes you and your teams have achieved while looking ahead and imagining how the future can be even better.

Once the C-suite executives have identified an area or areas in which teams need to be re-skilled, they can begin carefully selecting the technology or program best suited to their teams' needs. How will they know if the new tech or program they're putting into place is getting results? They must quantify the change they are implementing if it's going to provide any useful information.

Getting Buy-In from Your Teams

The second component of re-skilling your employees is getting buy-in from your teams. Any time you ask employees to change the way they operate, you open the door for significant pushback. If teams are constantly asked to change the way they do things because of the C-suite's whims, they will grow very frustrated indeed. That's why the first component is so important: Company leadership must agree on the value of the intended change so that employees will have more confidence in it as well.

Rarely do I see companies tie re-skilling as part of career development. Companies focus on the issue at hand. If team members can see how the new skill they're being asked to learn relates to the overall trajectory of their careers and ultimately the mission of the organization, they'll perceive the value in it. Hopefully, you as a people leader have a record of consistently showing your direct reports that you care personally, so they'll know you're interested in their growth. If you've been having conversations with them in which you dig into their big picture life goals, as we talked about in Chapter 9, you're halfway there already. Think about where your employees ultimately want to end up. Now, how will learning this new skill help get them there?

There must be a strong human element for individuals to trust the process. It should also be aligned with other talent management functions, not viewed as something extra that employees "have" to do, like homework. The C-suite must determine how urgent the needed change is. Does the entire sales force need to be re-skilled tomorrow? If the need is not extremely urgent, consider having employees opt in. You can incentivize it as you wish. Once these individuals begin to enjoy success, you can present them to your teams as case studies so that other employees are motivated to gain the new skill.

Ultimately, approach re-skilling with careful consideration for the desired impact on your organization and your teams. There's no need to bury your head in the sand, totally overwhelmed by all the new technologies available. Conversely, it's unwise to throw a bunch of things at the wall and see what will stick, which will only exhaust and frustrate your employees.

Technologies That Can Take You to the Next Level

We've discussed why it's important to continually re-skill your teams, and the two key steps in introducing and implementing a process change. Now I want to introduce you to three technologies that will help people leaders discover talent and fuel your teams' evolution to avoid dinosaur syndrome (falling behind in terms of the skill and functionality of your teams). Hopefully you won't feel overwhelmed when we're done. My goal is simply to direct you toward some extremely useful tech to explore that could streamline your processes and strengthen your operations while evolving your current talent in the organization. Let's walk briefly through each of them.

Bias Avoidance Talent Matching

The first tool is SquarePeg (https://www.squarepeghires.com), a matching service for job seekers and employers. SquarePeg uses online assessments to measure a candidate's aptitude, preferences, and character traits and determine which organization would be the best fit. Candidates take the assessment before they contact a recruiter (perhaps before they even formally begin their job search); they are then presented with a range of companies with whom they might enjoy working.

When founder Claire McTaggart was on my *EI Recruiter* podcast, she spoke of her time leading a recruitment team as a hiring manager for a strategy consulting firm. She found that her team was asking the wrong questions. Instead of, "Where did you go to school? What was your GPA? Which company are you at now?" they should have been asking "Do you enjoy solving analytical problems? Do you work well on teams? Are you interested in working with a large organization?"

The SquarePeg platform takes such psychometrics and preferences into account. How it works: The candidate takes the assessment, which matches her with jobs for which she is a strong fit. Each employer has already taken the assessment as well. When the candidate receives her report at the end of the assessment, it tells her, "You're an 84 percent match with Company XYZ, and here's why." She can then choose to connect with the companies she matched with. On the employer side, the hiring manager now has a curated selection of people who are a good fit for the organization and interested in working there. The recruiter gets to skip the tedious work of scanning through resumes and can focus on higher-value human-to-human exchanges, educating the candidate about the role and telling her where she may experience success as well as which job functions might prove challenging. The algorithms that match candidate with employer are bias-free; recruiters are sometimes influenced by prejudices in the traditional "six-second resume scan." The candidate may have her biases challenged as well; for instance, she might not want to work at a certain company because of a personal prejudice, but her job report suggests she'd be a perfect match. She has a chance to reconsider and perhaps embark on a truly rewarding opportunity. It's a win-win.

Predictive Machine Learning Evolving at the Speed of Your Organization

Pymetrics (https://www.pymetrics.com/employers) uses neuroscience and machine learning to help companies hire in a way that's predictive and diversity-friendly. Its creator, Frida Polli, a past guest on the *EI Recruiter* podcast, is a bit of a brainiac. With degrees from Dartmouth, Harvard, Suffolk University, and MIT, Frida had spent more than 10 years studying neuroscience in an academic setting. Yet when she began her MBA program to transition to the business world, she experienced the "problem" of recruiting for corporations on a firsthand basis. Everyone in her MBA program was looking for what came next after their degree. At the same time, Frida saw companies spending lots of money on recruitment technologies for little results. That's when her idea for Pymetrics came about.

A candidate encounters Pymetrics as the first step in a company's job application process. Pymetrics uses neuroscience games and machine learning to predict whether a candidate would be a good fit in the workplace. Here's how it works: The candidate takes a 20-minute assessment in the form of computer games that analyze things such as memory, planning, attention, risk tolerance, risk and reward profile, and learning style. Prior to this, everyone else in the company had taken the assessment, too. Pymetrics then compares the data from the assessments to determine whether the candidate is a good match.

There are three especially cool features of this technology:

1. *It is self-learning and adaptive.* As your organization's needs evolve, the tech can evolve with it. Pymetrics can anticipate the "future person" you'll need to move your company forward and test candidates to see if they fit that future role.

2. *It is designed to be bias-free.* All humans have biases, whether we want to admit it or not. When a recruiter scans resumes, a candidate is less likely to get an interview if said candidate is a woman, a person of color, older, etc. Pymetrics selects candidates via an unbiased algorithm; the recruiter can then focus on human-centered aspects of the work.

3. *If a candidate is not a good fit, it will direct him to other companies for which he might be better-suited.* I particularly love this last aspect; what a brilliant way to elevate employer brand. If candidates go through the application process and do not end up signing on with the company, they still leave happy—now they have all these other options! Organizations using the Pymetrics technology can thus communicate care for the individual candidate, even if he does not become a new hire.

Evolving Your Current Employees

Your current internal operations need to be evaluated, evolved, and invested in. The Riff Learning technology (https://www.rifflearning.com) has the potential to transform them. Cofounded by Beth Porter and legendary MIT professor and entrepreneur Alex "Sandy" Pentland, Riff measures conversational dynamics and provides feedback during and after video interactions.

What percentage of your business do you conduct via video-conferencing? Chances are it's a high number. Riff Learning works to enhance the satisfaction of participants in these conferences. In a meeting—whether in person or via videoconferencing—the goal is dynamic collaboration. You want an environment in which participants freely share ideas and opinions to arrive at authentic solutions. As a people leader, you want to know whether this collaboration is happening or whether one person is grandstanding and discouraging the participation of others, either consciously or subconsciously.

The Riff platform has three core features to make your video-conferencing as productive as possible. Riff uses the vocal activity and facial-gesturing patterns of participants to measure when people are talking, whether they are agreeing with each other, and participants' levels of engagement (it does this without recording the *content* of the conversations). It also offers real-time feedback through a feature called the "meeting mediator," which tracks "turn-taking" in the exchange and notes whether one person is dominating the conversation. Finally, after the meeting is over, Riff offers an analysis of your interaction and gives you a history of your interactions in past videoconferences.

For companies that do a significant portion of their business remotely, Riff is enormously beneficial. Conference participants who tend to take up most of the air in a conversation may not realize what they're doing. Conversely, less talkative participants may feel there is no opportunity for them to share their thoughts—they leave such meetings feeling frustrated and disengaged. Riff measures these dynamics in real time and provides the data to the employee so they are aware of the behaviors impacting collaboration and other team dynamics that are skewing in a less than optimal way. Riff values the contribution of *all* your team members—not just the loudest. By measuring participation and engagement, team members are invited to rethink their conversational dynamics and aim for more genuine collaboration.

The Bottom Line on Re-Skilling, Recruitment, and Tech

Technology is evolving at a pace we can't truly comprehend, and there is so much that still needs to be done. I'd like to see candidate-tracking systems upgrade faster. I'd like to see data scientists and ethicists working alongside HR departments. To get a little dreamy, imagine if future chief human resource officers actually had a background in ethics, organizational psychology, or philosophy. With the sum of prior experiences, they would be well-positioned to interpret future technology needs with a human lens and discern which adaptations would make the longest-term difference in the company's direction. They would help organizations avoid the trap of adopting technology with no clear sense of purpose, wasting time and money on a system that employees don't buy into and that muddles operations.

Whatever your organization's current status, you needn't see technological evolution as an elephant. When used correctly, tech can be a powerful unicorn-attraction tool. The situation is this: Remove the elephant to attract the unicorn—or become a dinosaur. Don't go extinct. Pick the tech that suits your needs, and re-skill your teams accordingly.

The Emotional Intelligence Factor

From an EQ lens, the imperative to re-skill your teams engages the *stress-management* component. Leaders are called on to be *flexible*, one of *stress management's* three pillars. They must adapt to the marketplace and be clear-eyed enough to see what's coming on the horizon, making necessary adjustments as they go. The *decision-making* component is also in play here. Its three subcategories are *reality testing, problem solving*, and *impulse control*. People leaders must first be centered enough to test their beliefs about the future with what is actually likely to happen. Then there is the problem solving: *Are we ready for coming changes in the field?* Leaders must then control their impulses to take hasty action and determine the best steps to lead their teams forward, ensuring that they have buy-in from direct reports to implement the needed changes.

From the *interpersonal* component, *empathy* is also hugely important. Recognize that many of your employees are likely fearful about the advancement of artificial intelligence and the rapid rate of technological evolution: *Will a robot take my job? Will I have to start all over again in a different field? How will I secure my future when so many jobs are moving to large metropolitan areas?* This is where the onus falls on you, a passionate people leader who cares directly about your employees. No one likes to be told what to do or to master a certain way of doing things only to be told that it is now obsolete. Put yourself in your direct reports' shoes. If someone were to tell you that *you* need to change the way you do your job, how would you like that information communicated? What assurances would you need? Wouldn't you want to know the value in gaining a new skill? Such questions will guide you well when you find yourself in this delicate position. There is never a reason to abandon your humanity.

> ## ▶ QUESTIONS FOR REFLECTION ◀
>
> You don't have to be a genius to figure out how to re-skill your teams. You simply need to acknowledge your biggest pain points. Ask yourself: Where could the job be easier? Where are your employees spending too much of their time? Turn inward first. Then seek the solution by asking:
>
> ▶ What is currently the biggest need in your company's HR tech stack (the technology tools and apps that help your HR ecosystem run) to solve these challenges?
>
> ▶ How can you gather the right people to probe this need and find solutions?
>
> ▶ What growth and organizational company values would be supported by additional HR tech stack investment?
>
> ▶ Which leaders can you bring on to be the brain trust of this digital evolution?
>
> ▶ Exercise in imagination: Write a press release on your new tech solution. Address these questions: How will it impact the candidate and employee experience? How will it increase your organization's potential?

Chapter 15

Elephant: You Resist Emerging Work Trends

I f you want to attract the top talent of today, you have to stop thinking like the people leaders of yesterday.

For example, what aspects of a working life do you consider a "given"? Do you believe that having a job means you're in the office every day from 9:00 A.M. to 6:00 P.M.? What's your expectation of paid time off (PTO)—ten days a year? More, if your time-off policy is especially liberal? What benefits automatically come with a full-time job? You likely expect that your company will offer a retirement plan—but what about help repaying student loans?

People leaders of any organization today find themselves helming a work force of unprecedented diversity. This diversity comes in several forms. There's the kind we discussed in Chapter 10—of gender, race, sexual orientation, etc. But age is also an area of increasing diversity. Baby boomers are living longer and working longer; three out of four Americans report that they plan to continue working past age 65. Millennials are maturing in their careers and rising to positions of leadership. Gen Z is entering the work force. Each generation brings its own expectations about what makes for meaningful work.

In this chapter, we will look at seven major work trends I have experienced with my Silicon Valley clients and their brand-name digital competitors for some time, although they might still be new to you. Some of these we've touched on in previous chapters, so this space will serve as a review. This chapter will also aim to give you a better picture of the work landscape from a candidate's point of view. From there, you can capitalize on whichever trend best aligns with your mission and vision.

Seven Emerging Work Trends You Should Be Paying Attention To

Work trends come and go—they are trends, after all. But some have staying power. I have noticed seven in particular in my work as an executive recruiter that indicate a move toward a new way of working. Any company looking to scale and stay relevant should pay attention to them. You shouldn't feel pressured to completely overhaul your company's "style" to attract unicorns, but you may recognize some things your organization is already doing well and lean into them. Since the world of work is increasingly diverse, your unicorns could be attracted by any one of dozens of attributes.

Flexible Working Hours

As a population, we're long past the concept of the 9-to-5, 40-hour workweek. The ubiquity of technology has resulted in most professionals

performing work functions outside working hours—in the evenings, first
thing in the morning, on the weekends, etc. In many ways, we've moved
past the need for a physical, central work space (though we haven't
outgrown the need for human interaction, as evidenced by the emergence
of shared work spaces). The gig economy has also elevated the role of
freelancers in large organizations. Thus, the boundaries between work and
other aspects of life have become even more porous.

Do your company policies recognize this flexibility? Professionals
increasingly expect their employers to offer benefits such as working
one day a week from home or flexible start and end times. For example,
Student Loan Hero, which helps recent grads organize, manage, and
repay student loans, has an entirely remote work force—*and they didn't
lose a single employee in their first five years,* as reported in a Gusto
article by Kinjal Dagli Shah. It's a truly mind-boggling statistic that
illustrates how flexible work arrangements communicate to your teams
that you value their time and trust them to do their work. Such a vote of
confidence goes a long way.

Emphasis on Financial Wellness

Speaking of student loans, according to Debt.org, the total U.S. student
debt currently stands at about $1.54 trillion. *Trillion.* A graduating
member of the class of 2016 owes on average more than $37,000 in student
loans, according to Ivy League executive coach Aviva Legatt. The crushing
student loan debt of American students in particular has been described as
a type of financial trauma. In an April 2018 *Business Insider* article, Judith
Ohikuare reported on companies that have realized that offering assistance
to workers with student debt gives them a competitive edge in the
marketplace. Companies like accounting firm PwC and fitness company
Peloton offer employees $100 a month toward their student loan principal.
A common trend is to cap payments at $10,000. If you have an employee
coming in with $30,000 in student debt who sees an opportunity to erase
$10,000 of it over seven years, that's *hugely* motivating. It's a brilliant
strategy that provides a win-win: debt relief for your team members and
employee retention for the organization.

Mental and Emotional Wellness Takes Center Stage

Besides student loan assistance, PwC is also leading the way in offering emotional and mental health assistance to its employees. Beth Taylor is the mental health leader at PwC. She has helped launch an initiative to name six PwC leaders as "mental health advocates." Struggling employees are encouraged to reach out to one of these advocates, who have been trained in empathy and nonjudgmental listening. As part of this initiative, PwC has begun "Green Light to Talk" days. Participants wear green ribbons to indicate they are available for conversation about the importance of mental well-being. The point is to destigmatize mental illness.

PwC is just one example of a company that has made mental wellness a priority. People leaders of today should be aware that younger workers have come of age with words like "mindfulness," "wellness," and "emotional health" as part of their lexicon. They're most likely accustomed to talking openly about their experiences in therapy, and yoga has never been an exotic concept for them. If you have any hang-ups about discussing mental and emotional health, you'd be wise to move past them and see how you can prioritize wellness in the workplace, or have someone else in company leadership drive such an initiative.

Timely Performance Reviews

In Chapter 8, we talked about the need for managers to deliver ongoing feedback to their direct reports. Feedback should be given as often as possible so that direct reports can course-correct as needed—or so they can receive affirmation for work well-done and be incentivized to do more. (Remember: Managers should be *receiving* feedback from their direct reports as well and must take the time to make this a regular feature of the workplace. This two-way communication establishes trust.)

More and more organizations are adopting this approach. The result: 8 to 12 percent of Fortune 500 companies have eliminated annual performance reviews (as of 2014) and 29 percent are thinking about eliminating them. Leaders at top organizations have expressed their frustrations with the old model. The yearly performance review creates excessive paperwork, restricts creativity, causes undue stress, requires a huge time investment for limited gains, etc. The primary difficulty with the yearly review is that it evaluates work done in the past, rather than focusing on how the team member can grow in the future. The tension between yearly performance review proponents and those who espouse the ongoing feedback model aligns with the fixed mindset vs. growth mindset debate. Do you believe that employees' talent is fixed—that "you get what you get" when you hire someone? Or do you value the potential in your direct reports and believe each could rise to positions of increased leadership and responsibility?

More companies are embracing a growth mindset these days, and that requires regular, ongoing feedback, which allows for quicker improvement and growth. If you're still doing a yearly performance review, I invite you to reconsider your methods. I truly believe it will soon be relegated to history.

Prominent Use of Artificial Intelligence

This shouldn't be a surprise to anyone. This is where the war for talent is especially hot; companies are courting AI engineers and tech specialists (and offering them exorbitant salaries) to compete. One example of AI becoming more commonplace in the work force is chatbots. When is the last time you interacted with a chatbot? Chances are it was very recently. Chatbots have become key for customer relations, and they will only become *more* prominent: In 2018, research and advisory company Gartner predicted that by 2021, 50 percent of enterprises will spend more on developing chatbots and other bots than mobile apps.

AI is the new electricity. It will revitalize almost every service available today. In Chapter 14, we looked at how new recruiting software uses artificial intelligence to match candidates with employers as well as to predict companies' future needs. Recruitment technology is one area in which AI is already front and center; there are now dozens of programs that will do the tedious work of scanning resumes. Today's recruiters can spend their time doing the human-centered work of educating candidates and working with hiring managers to meet current needs.

I mention recruiting to illustrate a larger trend: We needn't fear AI. Culturally, we're moving past the doom-and-gloom thinking that previously dominated any attempt to have a meaningful conversation about it (thank God). Humans working with AI systems have the power to advance society in ways that capture the imagination and inspire hope and excitement. CEOs and other people leaders still stuck in fear mode would do well to educate themselves and start dreaming about the possibilities.

Embracing an Aging Work Force

Over the past 100 years, we have increased our life expectancy by 50 percent. One result of this astounding achievement is that more workers are staying on the job past the "traditional" retirement age. There are a number of reasons for this. Older workers may be supporting children facing enormous student loan debts, or they may still be rebuilding retirement savings they lost in the 2008 recession. Many see no point in retiring at 65; they've attained status and respectability in their careers and remain healthy and interested in the work, so why quit for a retirement that could last decades?

How well does your workplace accommodate older workers? Are you actively working to prevent ageism in the office? Look to Germany to see what fighting ageism in the work force looks like. Car company Daimler has 136,000 employees; the average age is 44.7. Emma Thomasson, reporting for Reuters in June 2018, described how Daimler established an exhibit to bust stereotypes about age: Participants enter the exhibit through "young" or "old" doors, based on their personal feeling (not their actual age). Inside, they are tested on things like memory, grip strength, how high they can jump, etc. They are then given an "emotional age" and a "biological age." The exhibit is meant to show that many stereotypes of aging are out of date and that diversity of age means diversity of experience.

Also in Germany, tech company SAP runs a "mature talents" program, a two-way mentoring program between younger and older employees. It is designed to ensure that employees who are about to retire effectively transfer their knowledge to the next generation of workers.

In meeting the needs of older workers, communication is key. For example, absenteeism is a common problem with older workers that may be due in part to more physical ailments or chronic illness. It's important for people leaders to keep lines of communication open to understand *why* their older workers are absent (if this is, indeed, a trend in your company).

Could you make some simple modifications to their job functions or automate some tasks to ease physical strain? Would more PTO be attractive to your older employees?

Attracting and retaining younger employees is vital to your company's success, of course. Yet older employees represent a treasure trove of knowledge and experience. Looking to the needs of an aging work force so this knowledge can be used and ultimately passed on should be a facet of your strategic planning.

Increasing Reliance on Freelance Workers

Particularly in the U.S., the "gig economy" is huge. Caleb Gayle reported for *The Guardian* in June 2018 that 16.5 million Americans are working in "alternative" or "contingent" roles. That number is still just an educated guess; there's no way to know the exact percentage of the labor force working in freelance roles. Many people freelance as their primary means of employment, while others pick up side gigs like driving for Lyft or Uber in addition to their full-time jobs. Workers may opt in to the gig economy for many reasons: They see more earning potential than in a full-time job, they need a side hustle to pay off debts like student loans, they desire freedom and flexibility in their work schedules—the reasons are as varied as the individuals themselves. Whatever the causes of the gig economy's rise, it's not going away anytime soon. To ensure your processes run smoothly, you need to make accommodations for freelance workers to avoid continual interruptions whenever one employee leaves for another gig.

One way to do this is to create a remote, virtual workplace in which freelancers can learn the necessary skills fast. Managers also need to be able to continuously deliver feedback, even without the face-to-face, trust-building relationships that take place in an office.

Above all, you must embrace and attend to the needs of your freelancers. How you treat freelancers is as important to your employer brand as how you treat your full-time employees. Whatever you do, don't discount the contributions freelancers make to your company. Even though they don't have salaries, freelancers may prove to be some of your most valuable employees.

Creating the Workplace of the Future

PwC published a 2017 report, "Workplace of the Future," in which it attempted to analyze the work landscape of 2030, drawing on research conducted from 2007 to 2017. The report is rich and wide-ranging but can in essence be boiled down to a few key messages for people leaders:

▶ Act now: The future is here, and the rate of technological evolution is only accelerating.

▶ Recognize that the future is not "fixed": Plan for a dynamic rather than static future. Employ the motto "No regrets and bets."

▶ Go "bigger" and think in radical leaps rather than baby steps.

▶ Immerse yourself in the "automation debate." If you leave it to HR and technological specialists, you will be left behind.

▶ Protect people, not jobs. Nurture people's development through re-skilling; make adaptability a core virtue.

▶ Contextualize work with a clear narrative. Recognize that employees feel anxious about losing their jobs to automation; create open dialogue around this and continually include them in the story.

The report is worth reading in its entirety. In one especially interesting feature, researchers proposed four plausible futures for the work landscape of 2030:

1. A "gold" future in which humans come first, and social services/community-centered businesses prosper

2. A "red" future in which innovation rules, individuals and corporations race to give consumers the best products and services, and niche markets prosper

3. A "blue" future in which "corporate is king," and individual preferences take precedence over social responsibility

4. A "green" future in which "corporations care," and businesses take the lead in driving social change on issues like climate change and health care

Which future would you like to live in? How could you, as a people leader at your organization, with your team members and your particular set of opportunities and challenges, begin living in this future *right now*? The report urges, "This isn't a time to sit back and wait for events to unfold. To be prepared for the future, you have to understand it."

I tip my hat to that. "Emerging work trends" or "the future" in general needn't be seen as an elephant blocking your way. A more helpful analogy might be to view it as a wave to be ridden.

When you catch a good wave and ride its crest, picking up speed and distance the longer you stay up—so much faster and more thrillingly than your arms and legs could have ever taken you—true magic happens.

The Emotional Intelligence Factor

Adapting to emerging work trends is not easy. Change never is (for most of us, at least). People leaders poised to weather changes in the work force must engage fully the *decision-making* component of emotional intelligence. You must *problem solve*—one of the subcategories of *decision making*, which means you anticipate the needs of the market and pivot the company as required to meet them. You must also *test reality*, another pillar of *decision making*; it's imperative that people leaders be clear-eyed about the changing work landscape and see things as they really are. There's no sense in wishing for a bygone era or crossing your fingers in the hopes that things will continue exactly as they are. Successful people leaders are *always* looking to the future and trying to determine what's just around the bend. With astute observations and counsel from trusted business partners and mentors, you can anticipate shifts in the marketplace and change course as needed.

The *stress-management* component of EQ is also put to the test when adapting to the changing work landscape. *Flexibility* is a pillar of *stress management*. An effective people leader in the fourth industrial revolution can hold his plans and ideas in an open palm. He must be committed to success but flexible with the plans he will implement to achieve that success. People leaders must also stay *optimistic*, another pillar of *stress management*. This optimism is not a "pie in the sky," delusional sort of hope but one that is rooted in reality. That old saying is true: "Whether you think you can or you can't, you're right." Do you dread the future or anticipate it? Remember that if you're leading from a place of worry and stress, that negative energy will leak all over your company, and your forecast of doom will become a self-fulfilling prophecy. Even in the midst of vast upheaval and change, *you* can hold on to the practices and people who remind you of your essential humanity. Thus, you create spaciousness in your day, your week, and your life. (Go back and reread Chapter 13 if you need reminders on how to do this.)

▶ **QUESTIONS FOR REFLECTION** ◀

As a people leader, it's important to keep constant watch on the horizon. What does the future look like for your company? How can you stay ahead of the curve so you can recruit unicorns who can, in turn, help you enhance your company? Ask yourself and your team these questions:

▶ What kind of "future organization" are you creating, as defined by PwC? (See "Creating the Workplace of the Future" on page 140.)

▶ How are you fostering a feedback culture?

▶ How do you want your organization to stand out from a mental health and emotional wellness perspective?

▶ How will you prepare your organization for remote workers?

▶ How can you support your employees' financial wellness?

▶ Do you have a bias against flexible working hours? Examine and, if need be, reevaluate your attitude.

▶ How can AI help your organization compete?

▶ Is ageism (against older *or* younger workers) a problem in your workplace? If so, what are some creative ways you could counter it?

Chapter 16

Elephant: You Keep Attracting Fake Unicorns

You and your sought-after unicorn have made it official and signed on the dotted line. You both enjoyed a honeymoon period full of warm fuzzies and good feelings all around.

But then things began to change.

Your prized unicorn has started looking away when you try to make eye contact. He didn't hit his numbers last quarter. It's only been six months, but you have a sneaking suspicion your unicorn might be looking for the exit sign. What happens when you work *so hard* to get your unicorn, and it turns out he's just an ordinary horse?

In this chapter, we'll talk about why you may be attracting fake unicorns. If your new hires quickly lose their luster and the thrill of your partnership quickly morphs into the humdrum of day-to-day business, the problem may not lie with the unicorn. We'll take a look at how recruiting problems start with the company—not the candidate. And we'll show you how to bring more awareness to your processes. In this way, you become the unicorn you want to attract.

Recruiting Problem? First, Look in the Mirror

In his 2017 book *Recruit Rockstars*, Jeff Hyman states that only about half of new recruits meet their employers' expectations. That's a pretty crummy average, and yet most people leaders have faith in their ability to spot talent. Hyman says these self-professed "experts" trust their guts to a fault, so there is scant discussion on how to improve that average, and business continues as usual. It's hard to imagine other professions in which that rate of failure would be tolerated—imagine the uproar if 50 percent of cars that rolled off the assembly line were defective or 50 percent of high school graduates couldn't read.

It's clear that hiring managers and people leaders need to pause and reevaluate their methods. It's estimated that the cost of a bad hire can be 30 percent of the agreed-upon salary. So if you hire a supposed unicorn for $150,000 and she is gone in six months, which also prompts others to leave, calculate the financial loss and team morale challenges that will impact business performance. Can your company afford that kind of loss? What if it happens again and again and again?

The CEO, chief human resources officer, hiring manager, or any other people leader who keeps hiring "fake unicorns" needs to first look in the mirror to determine if *they* are the problem. We all have blind spots when it comes to hiring. Maybe a fake unicorn wooed a people leader with his Ivy League education. Or perhaps the CEO was buddies with the new hire's uncle and couldn't resist giving the kid a shot. We all over-identify with certain candidates for one reason or another. We keep rooting for them, hoping they'll live up to the idealized versions of themselves that we've created in our minds.

But missteps in hiring are just one reason your "unicorn" may have turned out to be a bust.

Let's work on your "fake unicorn" problem by assuming you're actually the source of the issue. Focus on what you can control—your own behavior—and let's look at some ways in which you may be sabotaging your unicorns' performance. In this chapter, I posit three ways in which people leaders may be unintentionally keeping their star hires from shining as brightly as they're capable of. We'll also look at ways to correct these patterns so your unicorns can live up to their potential.

You're Trusting Your Gut Too Much in the Hiring Process

As people leaders, we take pride in our ability to decide quickly and change our minds slowly. We trust our intuition and reasoning skills—and with good reason: These are the tools that have helped us rise to positions of prominence in our companies. The further up the ladder you go, the more you encounter leaders sure of their decision-making abilities. To a certain extent, this is all fine: Employees and shareholders lose faith in the mission if their leaders are constantly changing their minds with every gust of wind. Strong, decisive leaders with a clear sense of the best way forward are a boon to any organization.

Yet this attitude can be a stumbling block in hiring. When it comes to filling key positions, do you have a persuadable mind about candidates? Or do you tend to make a judgment in the first minute of an interview and stick to it?

I'm not talking about disregarding first impressions—we can't. We're biologically wired to size people up the instant we lay eyes on them. It's an instinct left over from a more dangerous time. *Is this person a friend or foe?* we ask ourselves. (Or, if this person's actually a saber-toothed tiger: Do I need to run *right now*?) We immediately make hundreds of little judgments as soon as we see someone: This person is like me or not like me, tall or short, thin or heavy, dressed fashionably or sloppy, etc.

Let's assume that all your unicorns come into their interviews in work-appropriate attire so we're not discounting anyone on the basis of

unprofessionalism. What we're talking about here is the interviewer—
you—relying too much on your judgment during and after the interview.
Consider these questions to see if you are perpetuating this dynamic:

- ▸ Do you have a tendency to talk more than you listen in an interview?
- ▸ If it's a panel interview that you and your colleagues discuss afterward, do you have a system by which these discussions take place?
  (If you outrank everyone else on the panel, realize that they'll defer
  to your judgment if you speak first—unless you have a system to
  mitigate this power imbalance.)
- ▸ Before making hiring decisions, do you gather input from *all*
  parties who might have valuable information? I mean everyone.
  Were you paying attention to how the candidate treated the receptionist—and did you get the receptionist's opinion? Did you call
  all references to garner insight from them rather than calling to
  confirm the decision at which you'd already arrived? What about
  the candidate's potential direct manager and teammates?
- ▸ Do you have an assessment tool designed to prevent bias to analyze
  the candidate's competencies, preferences, and potential?
- ▸ Are you very clear on what you want from the candidate?

The last bullet point seems obvious. But again and again, people
leaders get themselves into fixes because they're not sure what *exactly*
they want. They know they want a "superstar" who'll raise the level of the
organization, but they're uncertain about what being a "superstar" entails.
This is when they fall into the trap of being wowed by items on a resume
that turn out to mean very little. "This guy went to Harvard—surely he's
got what it takes!" Or, "She's an ex-Googler! Maybe she'll bring some of
that magic to our team."

It doesn't work that way. On a deeper level, we know better than to
be dazzled by an exclusive school or glamorous past employer. But in
the presence of impressive credentials, we have a tendency to act like a
worshipful fan at the Oscars. We're blinded by the flashbulbs, if you will—
unable to see if the candidate before us can actually fill the role we need her
to perform. We *especially* fall into this trap when we're not clear on what
we want that role to be.

So many hiring missteps can be avoided with some simple awareness. We must be aware of our biases and our areas of insecurity. We must be aware of which situations cause us to distort our view of the actual person sitting in front of us. Gut reaction is important, but it's far from the only thing that's important—especially when it comes to crucial decisions like hiring for key roles.

Technology can be your friend when making hiring decisions. If your company has not already implemented a talent filter designed to funnel the best candidates to your organization through assessments that are competence- and preference-based and bias-free, I recommend investing in one. (We discussed two such platforms in Chapter 14: Pymetrics and SquarePeg.) These tools can help ensure your workplace reflects the broader world rather than your own preferences. The more diversity in your office—of gender, race, sexual orientation, physical ability, age—the more creatively your company will think and the faster you can move forward.

Remember, what got you here won't get you there. If you pride yourself on decisiveness and intuition, you must still recognize how those instincts could be crippling your hunt for true unicorns. Be aware of your own unhelpful tendencies and get second opinions. Putting the brakes on and reexamining the way in which you hire could be the most helpful action you take toward attracting and retaining unicorns.

Your Unicorn Is in the Wrong Role

If your unicorn isn't performing the way you'd hoped, or you sense he is dissatisfied or unhappy, he may be in the wrong role.

You may balk at this. "How could he be in the wrong role? It's the job we hired him for!" Or, "I know he has the skills and can deliver on what we need. He's perfectly able to do the job. So how could it be the wrong role?"

There are all sorts of reasons a unicorn may find himself in the "wrong" role, even if it aligns perfectly with his skill set and experience. A role can be "wrong" if it is unduly stressful and takes too great a toll on his mental well being. It's "wrong" if it doesn't allow him to do the things that truly light him up. It's "wrong" if he is an extrovert, and the job requires him to be holed up in an office for most of the day away from the energizing presence of co-workers (or vice versa—if he's an introvert and is forced to interact with other people all day).

At this point, you may be thinking, "How can I possibly know their preferences, stress levels, personal life situation, etc.?"

This is where we come back to what we talked about in Chapter 8: You *must* know your direct reports. It's up to managers to have frequent conversations with their direct reports—both professional and personal in content—in which they learn the details of their lives: preferences, concerns, significant life events that may be on the horizon, etc. As a people leader, these conversations are never just idle chitchat—they are part of your job. You cannot hope to manage effectively and lead your team to new levels if you don't know who they are as individuals.

You may have noticed that your unicorns can be divided into two different camps. One group is hungry for every opportunity you can throw at them, asking about advancement from day one. I call these people "astronauts." Light the fuse, and they'll overshoot the moon.

The second group is content to stay in their roles. They value detail and mastery, becoming absolute experts in their area and setting the standard for everyone else. You can't run your organization without them; they build the foundation. I call this group "architects."

Architects are absolutely solid in their role; they have little or no interest in expansion and advancement. This could be because they have a lot going on at home, so they don't want to add more to their plates at work. Or maybe they have outside interests that are important to them—training for a triathlon, for example. For whatever reason (or no reason at all), architects are dedicated to their current role.

By contrast, astronauts are on a steep growth trajectory. They want every opportunity you can throw at them. If they don't advance quickly after coming aboard, they're likely to grow restless and begin looking for another position. They are "all in" from the beginning; it's up to their manager to give them appropriate opportunities to stretch their wings and take off.

You need both astronauts and architects. Neither is "better" than the other. Without your architects, where will other team members turn for advice? On whom would you rely to get the job done well? And without astronauts, how will you achieve the levels of success you're hoping to have? Who will move your company forward?

If this classifying system is helpful to you in identifying your team composition and the needs and wants of your employees, I invite you to use it. Ask yourself: What does this architect want? What incentives and rewards are attractive to her? She may have little interest in managing. Some companies reward architects by making them the "gurus" of their particular area of expertise. Would this be attractive to *your* architects? If not, how will you recognize their hard work and competence?

If you've got an astronaut, how will you keep her challenged and engaged? What new responsibilities will cause her to light up? Have conversations with her in which you chart out where she would like to be in six months, one year, etc., and then plot a course with her to achieve these goals.

Really, whether your new unicorn is an astronaut or an architect, you need to be having these career conversations with her—and with *all* your team members. When you make it a point to know your employees both professionally and personally, you'll be able to tell if they are unhappy. Remember, your team members probably don't want to upset you and therefore won't volunteer this information. Recognize that their happiness *is* your business. While you can't take responsibility for their emotions, you *can* get to know them and strive to make work a place where they are challenged, engaged, and enjoying themselves.

You're Unclear About What You Want

If your new hire comes in with a stellar resume, you may believe she requires little direction from you regarding your expectations. Maybe her role at her past company was very similar, and she knocked it out of the park. Perfect! You'll just plug her into the team, and she'll be off and running in no time.

Here's a tip: The best managers *never* try to skip out on communication with their direct reports. Even if you are introverted and feel slightly uncomfortable when talking about goals and how you will evaluate your team members' performance. Even if your new hire is exceedingly competent and could likely do the job blindfolded. Even if your schedule is already jam-packed, and you're relieved at having such a capable team member who apparently needs so little from you. Even if your new hire is actually Wonder Woman, and you're just a little bit awed by her.

Even if, even if, even if.

It's your job to clearly communicate expectations from the get-go. It's also your job to do everything in your power to *help* your new hire meet those expectations. Don't make the mistake of skimping on communication because you've signed a star player. In fact, star players often benefit the *most* from direct coaching. Your unicorns are looking to grow and improve. They bring their A game to work. If you try to meet them with your C game, your unicorns are going to get frustrated very quickly, and they won't stick around very long.

No matter how well your new hire performed in her previous role, there will always be a learning curve. She is surrounded by a new team with different working styles. Your organization may use different technology than what she is used to. Perhaps your company's work culture is more demanding than her previous environment. Whatever the differences, your unicorn needs coaching if she is going to achieve her highest potential. It's your job to make sure she is clear on what she's doing, making appropriate progress, and settling into her new role.

Put Yourself in Your New Recruits' Shoes

Few things are worse than pouring your heart and soul into something and being met with ambivalence from your superiors. That's why it's important for you to over-communicate with your direct reports. They need to know your expectations and be rewarded when they meet them. It's incredibly discouraging for employees to feel as if their managers aren't really there. Nothing is as disheartening as working hard on deck, only to discover that no one is steering the ship.

Take the time to do some internal check-ins, in which you ask yourself:

▶ Do I know what our goals are?
▶ Have I communicated those goals clearly?
▶ How is each member of my team doing?

▸ Do I *know* that's how they're doing—have I talked to each individual lately?

The more you know yourself, the better you'll be at attracting and retaining star talent. This is true on both an organizational and an individual level. The company must be clear about its purpose and goals—its "why." People leaders must be clear on their strengths and weaknesses, how they communicate, and how they get things done. To put a slightly more metaphysical spin on it, you attract what you already are. If you or your organization is confused about your work or how you do it, you're at a disadvantage when it comes to getting a unicorn. You're just praying to get *someone* who can do the work. But that someone may not be a unicorn, even if she hails from Harvard or Facebook or wherever. And if she *is* the unicorn you're after, she is not going to stay in a job that is muddled, answering to managers who are unclear in their expectations—and who therefore undervalue her talents.

CASE STUDY
Finding the Perfect Mix of Unicorns

Jeffrey, the principal data science manager at a major tech corporation, was in charge of assembling a team to develop and implement a mixed-reality application to measure how people use the company's tools in the workplace. He knew he wanted data scientists on the project from its inception, but that posed a problem: How do you bring data scientists onboard when there *isn't yet data?*

Jeffrey knew he would need team members with a diverse set of skills for the project to succeed. He needed five core people for his team as well as a project manager. He could have taken the usual route, which would be to choose four team members deeply versed in the subject material—e.g., four machine learning engineers or four experts in data visualization. But Jeffrey wanted the team to be able to solve the puzzle posed by the project. He wanted people who could imagine what would be useful to learn from the data and then figure out how to measure it. The project would most benefit from having the team members viewing that puzzle through four separate (yet compatible) lenses, so Jeffrey was after people with diverse backgrounds and expertise.

So he set about assembling his team. One team member came from an operations research background and had strong statistics and coding skills. Another was very new to data science but had a deep mathematics background and ten years of experience as an educator. A third was a designer specializing in visualization who also held advanced degrees in computational biology. Two data engineers rounded out the crew—one with experience "productionizing" data and the other with a background in "fuzzy data mining."

The most important skill Jeffrey was looking for in his team members was the ability to *tell a story*. To create a compelling product, he knew he needed people with strong communication skills. The interview he created contained questions to evaluate how well the candidates could communicate. Jeffrey asked them to explain algorithms to him "as if I were in fifth grade." Could they break down complex processes and operations so they were understandable to people with absolutely no experience in the subject? How did they deploy analogies? Was the picture the candidates painted vivid and enticing?

Even though Jeffrey's job is all about data, he resists being labeled as "data-driven," finding it devoid of humanity and lacking room for the ineffable qualities that exist *behind* the data. He says it's easy to see *what* is happening—what's difficult is understanding *why*. Jeffrey prefers "data-informed," meaning that the team is reflecting on the significance of the data they're gathering.

That's why assembling a team of storytellers was so important to him. Jeffrey wanted emotionally intelligent team members who could deploy their empathy and understand the intent behind the questions. He wanted people who could get to the root of a problem and ask, "What is it you're *really* curious about? Never mind about the data—we'll figure out the quantitative part later." Thus, his team would use their imaginations to design a product that would eventually yield them valuable information.

Jeffrey joined a leadership team that was fully formed with the exception of the data role he filled and was tasked with assembling his team in a mere eight weeks. In that time, he reviewed hundreds of resumes, which he eventually culled down to five. He had to find his team members and prepare them for the task under an incredibly tight deadline.

Fortunately, the rest of the leadership team was already sold on the value a data team would bring. It wasn't a question of "Why do we need that?" but "When do they get here?" Thus, Jeffrey could focus solely on building his team for those eight weeks. The pressure was immense, but he was fully supported in his mission and able to attract the unicorns he needed.

So what can we learn from Jeffrey's experience?

Jeffrey had a clear vision for what he wanted from his team: storytellers with diverse backgrounds and experiences who could imagine the role of data from the inception of a product. He knew exactly what he was looking for, so he wasn't dazzled by fancy degrees or job titles. Depth of experience and emotional intelligence were the most important factors. He was clear on his needs, and he communicated those with his team. He was also committed to their development—how everyone on the team might work together to increase one another's skill sets. Jeffrey set expectations from the beginning so the data scientists wouldn't grow frustrated with the early lack of data.

And what greased the wheels, so to speak, for the successful assembling of the team? The backing of leadership, who gave Jeffrey the directive to focus solely on finding the right people. With enough support, stellar teams can be created—even in a hurry.

The Emotional Intelligence Factor

When attracting unicorns, the *self-perception* component of EQ-i 2.0 is put to work. To get the talent you want and need, first work on yourself. The company and the individual people leader must have a strong sense of *self-regard.* They must be working toward *self-actualization,* ever on the road to improvement. And the individual or company needs *emotional self-awareness*; emotions should be recognized and expressed, but strong emotions should not drive important decisions.

In retaining unicorns, the *interpersonal* component of emotional intelligence is key. People leaders must take great care to cultivate *interpersonal relationships* that are satisfying to all team members. The key for Jeffrey's team was to find people who could work together well and thereby improve the quality of work for everyone.

Relationships can be cultivated by continual conversation, both professional and personal, in which you and your direct reports share of yourselves. People leaders should always use their *empathy* in these relationships. It doesn't take much; just put yourself in the shoes of your team members and imagine how they may be feeling, what their needs might be, where there have been gaps in communication lately, and so on.

To avoid falling for a "fake" unicorn, go beyond your gut—gather the input of anyone and everyone who could shed light on the character and abilities of your candidates. To get the best out of a true unicorn, be absolutely clear on your wants and needs, and over-communicate those to him. Then make sure you know what *he* wants and work to see that he is getting opportunities that excite him and that work is a happy place for him to be. In the end, most of this work falls on you, the people leader. That should come as a relief since, ultimately, you are the only thing you can control.

▶ QUESTIONS FOR REFLECTION ◀

Everyone makes hiring missteps. Banging your head against the wall and bemoaning your poor judgment does no good. What's important is that you learn from the experience and enter the next hiring phase with more self-awareness. I invite you to reflect on the last "fake unicorn" you onboarded and ask yourself:

- ▶ Why did you believe this person was going to be a star?
- ▶ What went wrong?
- ▶ What was your part in it? (Were your expectations unclear? Were you dazzled by the companies they had worked for? Or, a fancy degree? Blinded by familiarity?)
- ▶ Were there any warning signs you can see in hindsight but which you failed to heed when it counted?
- ▶ How can you avoid making the same mistake again?

Self-reflection will only get you so far; accountability will take you the rest of the way. Ask your most trusted colleagues to keep you accountable as you work to move past your biases and hire unicorns who will contribute to the greater good.

Chapter 17

A Better Way to Handle Your Elephants

We've spent the last 16 chapters looking at mistakes organizations make that create confusion, drive talent away, and frustrate the talent they already have—the elephants standing in the way of the unicorns. There are many, many ways organizations and people leaders can go wrong and frustrate their best efforts. But now we're going to shift focus and look at one organization that's getting it right. *Really* right.

I had the honor and joy of speaking at the World Bank in the spring of 2018. Right away, I felt at home. I was thrilled to be surrounded by so many people dedicating their lives to making the world a better place. These, I felt, were *my* people—individuals who choose to embrace hope over cynicism. World Bankers are working daily to ensure that disadvantaged people all over the world can have security and opportunity. It was wonderful to be in their company and to learn from them.

The World Bank has institutionalized caring for its employees and their spouses. Built into its HR practices is respect for the basic dignity of each employee. Its policies are designed to nurture the whole individual— *not* just to "help them do their job" better. In this chapter, we'll look at how the World Bank's care for its employees frees them to wholeheartedly serve the world's most vulnerable people. The organization provides a clear road map for how to not only overcome elephants but also position your company as a unicorn magnet.

Institutional Caring

As dedicated as the employees of the World Bank are to improving the lives of the world's citizens, so is its leadership committed to improving the lives of the employees. When I learned of the benefits that come with a position at the World Bank, I was bowled over. Following are some of the particulars that blew me away.

Policies That Support Employees' Personal Needs

Employees at the World Bank are paid generously and given an excellent pension plan. Their relocation costs are covered. They're given 26 days of annual paid leave a year and 15 sick days; mothers also get three months of paid maternity leave and fathers get 10 days of paternity leave. That's a far cry from most U.S. companies that give ten days of paid leave a year and no parental leave. (In 2019, such ridiculous parental leave policies should no longer be on the books. In Canada, either parent may take a year. The U.S. has a lot of catching up to do to match the rest of the developed world in supporting new parents in the work force.)

The World Bank provides a state-of-the-art fitness center and an on-site health center for employees. There are on-site child care and lactation rooms for nursing mothers. "Work-life balance" isn't just given lip service at the World Bank. Company leadership has gone the extra mile to ensure the World Bank is caring for the whole employee.

Some may look at the World Bank's benefits and deem it all "too expensive." Certainly not every company can afford on-site health facilities or a child-care center. And yet, could your organization offer more paid leave? Could you be doing more to support new parents? Take even small steps to care more for your employees. When employees feel trusted and valued, they stick around. So the "expense" in creating that extra human touch—in caring for the *whole* employee, not just the "profitable" part—is returned tenfold when employees stick around and do their best work for you.

Support for Spouses *When an Employee Relocates*

The World Bank doesn't just care for its employees. As anyone in a committed partnership knows, when one person takes on a new job, *both* partners are actually signing on. They are agreeing to possibly changing their lives: moving, disrupting their current jobs and rhythms, making new child-care arrangements, etc. Moving for a partner's job—even if it's a once-in-a-lifetime opportunity—can be extremely stressful. The couple is leaving behind friendships and routines that they've presumably spent a long time establishing. Say it's a husband and wife and they're relocating for the wife's new job. If the husband had a job he enjoyed and to which he was committed, how will he fill the void in its absence? He may potentially lose out on much more than income.

I experienced this myself when my husband and I relocated to Vancouver for his new job at Electronic Arts. Let me be clear: I *love* Vancouver. When the opportunity came, I told my husband he had to take it. I'd always wanted to live in Vancouver, and here was our chance!

Yet even though the decision was easy, carrying it out was difficult. Change always is. I found myself in a new city with a toddler without knowing what my professional future held. My husband had his work to structure his days. I just had lots of questions. I was lonely and uncertain, even in a city I'd always wanted to call home.

Now imagine if EA had treated me the way the World Bank takes care of its employees' partners. It offers them membership in the World Bank

Family Network (WBFN), a volunteer group of spouses and partners of World Bank employees whose mission is to "welcome, support, empower, and advocate" on behalf of World Bank families. They host monthly information sessions in which World Bank employees and spouses can meet one another and learn about WBFN benefits. WBFN also holds spouse/partner orientations four times a year and "Navigating Culture Shock" seminars two to three times a year, where World Bank employees and spouses can learn about life in Washington, DC and the culture of World Bank. In addition, WBFN supports employees' partners who want to develop professionally through a number of career-oriented groups. There are clubs for teens, clubs that visit museums, clubs for mothers with toddlers—WBFN has, in the course of its 46-year history, thought of everything.

Imagine the stress that is alleviated with this type of support. World Bank employees and their families aren't simply *told* that they're valued: They're *shown* it from the very beginning.

Clarity of Mission

The World Bank has two main goals: to "end extreme poverty and promote shared prosperity in a sustainable way." With a mission like that, the World Bank attracts a lot of golden souls. People come to work there because they are savvy, pragmatic do-gooders who want to make a tangible difference in the world.

Obviously, you can never *really* know a company from the outside, just like you can never know someone else's marriage. Yet during my time at the World Bank, I was continually impressed by the energy and enthusiasm of its employees. They seemed truly happy and enlivened by their work. Employees are drawn in by the mission, and then they are taken care of so very well. My experience left me thinking—what if *every* organization had such cheerful ambassadors?

Your company may not be the World Bank. Perhaps your mission is less noble than ending poverty. Yet there is some nobility in the work you're doing. You see its importance, and you're motivated to do it well. (If not, it's time for a career change!) On a personal level, you may need to spend some time reconnecting to your "why." Leaders who are connected to their *why* are compelling; they inspire their teams and attract passionate, like-minded people. Then this same reconnection needs to happen on an organizational level. The mission statement should be common parlance in the office. Decisions should be evaluated in light of whether they line up with the stated mission of the organization.

Is your mission explicitly stated somewhere in your workplace? Are the employees familiar with it? Could they recite it at the drop of a hat? Does your mission have a bearing on your day-to-day operations?

What a Strong Mission Can Look Like

For an example of one company that knocks this out of the park, let's look at LinkedIn. LinkedIn's mission is "connecting the world's professionals to make them more productive and successful." LinkedIn also has a vision—though some CEOs use "mission" and "vision" statements interchangeably, LinkedIn CEO Jeff Weiner is critical of this practice. He believes (and has stated publicly) that companies should use a vision statement as a "true north," a guidepost that the organization is continually aiming for; the mission statement is the way in which that vision is achieved. LinkedIn's vision statement is "creating economic opportunity for every member of the global work force."

In addition to the mission and vision, six core values shape LinkedIn's culture. They are:

1. Members first
2. Relationships matter
3. Be open, honest, and constructive
4. Demand excellence
5. Take intelligent risks
6. Act like an owner

These are not just platitudes. Any person working at LinkedIn could recite the core values if stopped in the hallway. LinkedIn employees look to these values every week, every day, every hour—they are the guideposts that help workers find their way through difficult situations. The core values help everyone, from leadership to entry-level employees, keep to the mission at hand.

If a company is going to have a positive culture, everyone must know what they're shooting for. Organizations need agreed-upon rules that drive decisions and behaviors; these rules need to come from the top, and they need to benefit *everyone* (not just the C-suite).

Weiner talked about his approach of compassionate leadership in his 2018 commencement speech for the Wharton School.

Weiner says he *used* to manage people by hounding them with questions and growing frustrated when they did things differently from the way he would have done them. Instead of listening, he would be thinking of how to respond. Instead of inspiring people, this approach just frustrated and exhausted them. He realized something needed to change.

Weiner went on to say,

> *That meant pausing, and being a spectator to my own thoughts, especially when getting emotional. It meant walking a mile in the other person's shoes and understanding their hopes, their fears, their strengths, and their weaknesses. And it meant doing everything within my power to set them up to be successful.*

Weiner went on to explain that at LinkedIn, he's worked to create a culture with a "compassionate ethos." Leadership and employees are aligned around the mission; they trust one another and approach the work with the assumption that everyone has good intentions. As a result, LinkedIn leadership and team members can make important decisions very quickly. They don't waste time with office politics. Weiner added, "Create the right culture, and you create a competitive advantage."

People First

Jeff Weiner is a prime example of an emotionally intelligent CEO. He has learned how to observe his thoughts and emotions rather than be controlled by them. He can express his emotions without making others responsible for them; he is assertive without being domineering. Weiner has developed strong interpersonal relationships with his team members and has built a culture with an ethos of shared problem solving and responsibility. Any people leader looking to build an emotionally intelligent, resilient organization in advance of the fourth industrial revolution would do well to follow his example.

What the World Bank and Jeff Weiner have in common is prioritizing people. World Bank leadership and Weiner realize that their people are their most valuable asset. Caring for the needs of employees—physical, emotional, self-actualization, etc.—requires empathy as well as empathy in action (or "compassion," as Weiner puts it). People leaders must put aside their own egos and work for the good of the whole. If this attitude of serving leadership is present at the highest levels, the fruits are evident throughout *every* level. When people feel safe and supported—when there is basic trust and good feeling in the workplace—they feel free to be creative, to take risks, to form close relationships, to speak their minds. In that freedom lie the seeds of innovation that will take your organization forward.

The best investment you will ever make is in your people.

Chapter 18

Where We're Heading

The fourth industrial revolution is at our doorstep. It advances each day, whether or not we're prepared to meet it. Recall the McKinsey report cited in the introduction: The people who will prove the most resilient amidst the advance of artificial intelligence will be those who have developed their emotional intelligence. Emotionally intelligent people (and corporations) *are* the future of the work force.

The International Data Corp. (IDC) reports a $35.8 billion AI spend in 2019 alone, a 44 percent increase from 2018, and is expected to exceed the annual compound growth rate of 38 percent across five years. AI's capabilities are constantly expanding and creeping into every conceivable industry from shopping to defense, healthcare, fraud analysis, manufacturing across government, personal and consumer services, and education. AI will undoubtedly continue to rise. Yet it works best when it is guided by humans. For all its advantages, AI still gets many things wrong. We've all read alarming reports of AI systems that have learned to discriminate on the basis of race, sex, zip code, or other delineators.

We need good human intelligence directing artificial intelligence. We need individuals who are committed to evolving their EQ. We need people leaders with advanced emotional intelligence at the helm of conscious organizations that are dedicated to serving the greater good—of their employees and the world as a whole. If we add AI into this picture, my hope is that our capabilities will increase exponentially. Then there's no telling the amount of good we'll be able to do.

Artificial Intelligence: Neither Good Nor Bad

Are you excited about a world in which AI proliferates? I can see the potential, so I err on the side of excitement. There is so much opportunity before us. I believe that the rise of AI will create a world in which humans are free to do richer, more meaningful work.

Collectively, we as a society have wasted a lot of time debating if AI is "good" or "bad." Yet reality is always so much more interesting than dull binary terms. In truth, each stage of human evolution has created enormous opportunities, but it's also true that we've lost things we couldn't have imagined. The widespread adoption of agriculture meant we had more food, but we also went from carefree hunter-gatherers to people who stayed in one spot and worked long hours. Was that good or bad? The industrial revolution brought us from the farms to the cities. We created new technologies that harmed the environment, but they also increased the worldwide store of knowledge and connected people across the globe in previously inconceivable ways. Did we lose or gain?

The Future Is What You Make It

It's all in how you look at it. Yet I'm of the opinion that it does no good to stand around bemoaning progress and longing to return to a "simpler" time (whatever that might mean to you). It's better to spend your energies adapting to the needs of the modern work force—increasing your emotional intelligence so you and your organization can sidestep the elephants in your path and reach the unicorns who can move your company forward.

As a people leader, you face a unique challenge: the need to hire talent for roles that don't exist yet. A new technology could emerge tomorrow that disrupts the way we do everything. How do you enlist unicorns to help you prepare for such an uncertain future? How do you stay current and competitive? If Agile teams that are able to respond quickly to change are the way forward, how should you go about building and supporting those teams?

From the time a candidate first makes contact with a recruiter to the time she's worked in the job for a decade, your new hire, employee, architect, astronaut, or any other label you give her must be valued and supported. This can only happen in an emotionally intelligent organization. The recruiter takes the time to listen and value her needs above his own. The hiring manager helps create an engaging and relevant onboarding process. Managers regularly invest in their direct reports, giving them feedback and receiving feedback from them in return. They show their direct reports that they care about them as individuals, and with trust established, they offer feedback to move their team members forward. CEOs strive to ensure their workplaces are safe for all, not just those who come from privileged subsets of the population. Leaders make time for reflection and remain coachable—no matter how long they've been in their positions. They prioritize people over jobs and re-skill their teams when necessary with the buy-in of those teams. All people leaders keep one eye on the future so they can adapt their workplace as necessary.

It is my great hope that this book has helped you identify ways in which you can grow your awareness, develop your EQ, and help your organization clear the elephant herd standing between you and the unicorns you seek. The goal is not perfection but awareness and continual improvement. There is no perfect person or company. There are only emotionally intelligent humans doing the best we can, caring for our work and for one another, and striving to create the world in which we all want to live.

Step by step, we all move forward.

Acknowledgments

*E*lephants *Before Unicorns* could not have happened without the two Jennifers in my life. The first is Jennifer Dorsey, my wonderful editor. Thank you for responding to the manuscript with such enthusiasm and for your guidance on how to make this work pop in a traditional book publishing world. Sincere gratitude to Jennifer Locke, who has been on my editorial journey for more than a year. With great appreciation for Karen Billipp and Wyn Hilty for the precision editing at the very last editing hurdle.

I also want to take the opportunity to thank all the people who made this book possible, including Darrell West, vice president of governance studies at the Brookings Institution, for agreeing without hesitation to write the foreword. Thanks to Alfred Hermida at the University of British Columbia and Rachel Nixon, digital media visionary, for listening to my original book concept and helping me realize I needed a bigger idea and approach. Many thanks to Dorie Clark, author of *Entrepreneurial You,* who introduced me to Lucy McCauley, who became my first book coach. If it wasn't for Lucy's initial spark of enthusiasm and guidance, I wouldn't have started the intrepid journey of writing my first book.

Many thanks to all the people who assisted me along the way in making this book possible, including Jason Vantomme at Microsoft, Yvonne Quahe at the World Bank, Marshall Goldsmith, my EQ-i 2.0 trainer David Cory at The Emotional Intelligence Training Company, fellow emotional intelligence coach Nicole Gravagna for her constant real talk, my finance people Jerry Wong and Pat Barradas. Thank you to Chiara D'Avanzo, and Amy Metherell for holding down the fort at The FORWARD Co. when I was focused on *Elephants Before Unicorns.* This book wouldn't have been possible without insights from my group of amazing executive coaches and organizational consultants who, knowingly or unknowingly, keep me in check and inspire me, including Aviva Hirschfeld Legatt, Shira Miller, Kacey Cardin, Ali Davis, Jennifer Fondrevay, Marie Incontrera, Ron Carucci, Adele Gambardella-Cehrs, Tassey Russo, Marlena Corcoran, and Albert DiBernardo. Everyone needs at least one coach in their life—I'm lucky to have a great many influences!

And thank you to Daniel Goleman and all the emotional intelligence pioneers who put in decades of research to make emotional intelligence part of today's daily discussion.

About the Author

Caroline Stokes is a human capital entrepreneur helping everyone move forward in the fourth industrial revolution. She founded FORWARD, an executive headhunting and executive coaching company designed for global innovation leaders, and hosts the *Emotionally Intelligent Recruiter* podcast and learning platform to help recruiters evolve in the AI age. She currently resides in Vancouver.

Index